THE BEST freezer COOKBOOK

FREEZER FRIENDLY RECIPES, TIPS AND TECHNIQUES

THE BEST freezer COOKBOOK

FREEZER FRIENDLY RECIPES, TIPS AND TECHNIQUES

Robert ROSE

THE BEST **Freezer** COOKBOOK

For complete cataloguing information, see page 8.

DESIGN, EDITORIAL AND PRODUCTION:	MATTHEWS COMMUNICATIONS DESIGN INC.
PHOTOGRAPHY:	MARK T. SHAPIRO
ART DIRECTION, FOOD PHOTOGRAPHY:	SHARON MATTHEWS
FOOD STYLIST:	KATE BUSH
PROP STYLIST:	CHARLENE ERRICSON
MANAGING EDITOR:	PETER MATTHEWS
INDEX:	BARBARA SCHON
COLOR SCANS:	POINTONE GRAPHICS

We acknowledge the financial support of the Government of Canada through the Book Publishing Industry Development Program (BPIDP) for our publishing activities.

Published by: Robert Rose Inc. • 120 Eglinton Ave. E., Suite 1000

Toronto, Ontario, Canada M4P 1E2 Tel: (416) 322-6552

Printed in Canada

1234567 BP 04 03 02 01

contents

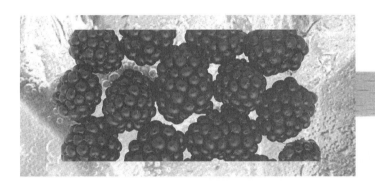

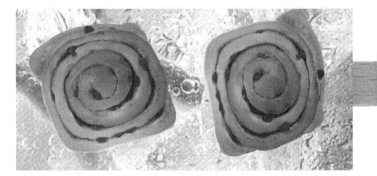

Contributing Authors

JULIA AITKEN, author of the *Easy Entertaining Cookbook*, is a leading food writer and cookbook author with more than 20 years of experience. Currently food editor of Elm Street magazine, her guests rarely cancel when she entertains.

In the *Easy Entertaining Cookbook*, Julia provides over 125 elegant-but-easy recipes, helpful tips and kitchen wisdom, as well as refreshingly frank advice on how to ensure a successful dinner party. (Rule #1: Only invite people you like.) Put that together with a great selection of flavorful dishes and you've got the perfect recipe for years of relaxed, enjoyable entertaining. Recipes from this book are found on pages 62 and 129.

JOHANNA BURKHARD, author of *The Comfort Food Cookbook*, is one of Canada's leading food writers. A former food columnist at the Montreal *Gazette*, she has been a regular contributor for over a decade to many national magazines, including *Canadian Living*, *Homemaker's*, *Wine Tidings* and *Elm Street*. Her most recent book is *Fast & Easy Cooking*.

The Comfort Food Cookbook is all about food that's simply, satisfyingly delicious. That's comfort food – and here's a book that features over 125 fast, easy-to-prepare recipes for the most comforting dishes you've ever tasted. A portion of the proceeds from each sale goes to the Children's Miracle Network. Recipes from this book are found on pages 48, 50, 51, 52, 90, 92, 176 and 178.

DIETITIANS OF CANADA, *Great Food Fast*, with authors Bev Callaghan, RD, and Lynn Roblin, M.SC., RD. Dietitians of Canada is the national voice of dietitians, working to improve the health of Canadians through food and nutrition. Bev is an experienced food writer and dietitian who has written frequently for a number of national magazines. Lynn has worked as a public health nutritionist before becoming an independent nutrition consultant and writer.

With *Great Food Fast*, you'll discover that good nutrition doesn't require a lot of work – and it tastes great! Recipes from this book are found on pages 53, 64, 91, 97, 102, 174, 175.

MARILYN CROWLEY AND JOAN MACKIE, co-authors of *The Best Soup Cookbook*. Marilyn is a professional chef, food writer and editor, most recently Associate Food Editor of *Chatelaine* magazine. Joan is an experienced journalist who has written hundreds of articles on food, lifestyle and home decorating for magazines in North America and overseas.

With *The Best Soup Cookbook* you will find recipes that you are sure to use again and again. They're easy to make and most can be prepared with ingredients found in your local supermarket. Recipes from this book are found on pages 42, 43, 44, 45, 46, 47 and 138.

BILL JONES AND STEPHEN WONG, co-authors of *New World Noodles*. Bill is a food consultant who works with Vancouver-area restaurants such as Sooke Harbour House. He also promotes B.C. food products in China and has wide-ranging experience in Asian and North American cuisine. Stephen is a Vancouver-based restaurant consultant and food writer. Bill and Stephen also collaborated on *New World Chinese Cooking*.

Everyone loves the simplicity of pasta. And now there's something even better. *New World Noodles* brings a fresh approach to mealtime, blending Eastern and Western flavors to give you over 100 tantalizing dishes. Best of all, these recipes are easy to make and can be prepared with widely available ingredients. A recipe from this book is found on page 68.

ROSE MURRAY, author of *Quick Chicken*, is an established food writer and author of more than half a dozen cookbooks.

With *Quick Chicken*, you can enjoy more than 135 different ways to prepare chicken – all in record time. Rose provides a wealth of tips, techniques and meal-planning ideas to accompany her inventive chicken recipes. If you love chicken (and millions do), there's no better book than *Quick Chicken*. Recipes from this book are found on pages 74, 75, 76, 86, 87, 89, 94, 100, 104 and 106.

Dedication

To my parents,
Jim and Alexa,
for their patience and support

Acknowledgements

Many thanks to Lesleigh Landry for her careful testing, editing and suggestions. You made it all possible!

– J. M.

National Library of Canada Cataloguing in Publication Data

Main, Jan
    The best freezer cookbook

Includes index.
ISBN 0-7788-0034-2

1. Cookery (Frozen foods) 2. Frozen foods. I. Title.

TX828.M33 2001   641.5'55   C2001-900968-2

freezer essentials

Freezing is the simplest, quickest form of food preservation. It doesn't require the purchase of any special equipment – since most people already have some type of freezer, whether it's a compartment in the refrigerator, or a stand-alone chest freezer in the basement. Above all, freezing is safe and convenient, allowing you to keep your favorite foods for months until you're ready to enjoy them. It's ideal for today's busy lifestyle.

How freezing preserves food

All food, raw or cooked, contains bacteria and other microorganisms (such as molds and yeast) that grow quickly at room temperature, causing the food to spoil. Freezing drastically slows the growth of these bacteria as well as other changes (see below) that affect the quality of food. Keep in mind, however, that freezing does not actually kill microorganisms; once the food is thawed, the bacteria become active again.

In addition to microbial growth, food spoilage can be caused by a number of other factors. These include:

Enzymes. All foods contain various types of enzymes – natural chemical agents that cause changes in color, texture, odor and flavor. Fruits and vegetables are particularly rich in enzymes, which must therefore be deactivated if the food is to maintain top quality while frozen. This is done by blanching (quickly boiling then cooling) vegetables or, in the case of fruit, adding ascorbic acid. See pages 25 to 29 in the next chapter for more information on these techniques.

Dehydration. All food is subject to dehydration or moisture loss which changes its texture and flavor. While this process is slowed down by freezing, it still takes place – particularly when foods are not wrapped properly. See "Packaging for the Freezer" (page 12), for more information on avoiding "freezer burn."

Oxidation. While we all need oxygen to live, it also has the effect of accelerating the discoloration and decay of food. Freezing foods – again, making sure it is thoroughly wrapped – helps to minimize this action.

Foods you shouldn't freeze

As a rule, the best foods for freezing are the freshest and best quality. Keep in mind that freezing will not improve the quality of food!

Remember, too, that freezing will not reverse the effects of spoilage – for example, perishable foods such as cream-based dips and spreads that have been left out at room temperature for several hours. These should be thrown out.

While freezing is an excellent method of preserving a wide variety of foods, there are some that are less suited to freezing than others. Some examples are shown in the table below.

FOODS NOT TO FREEZE	WHY	COMMENTS
Mayonnaise	separates	use whipped salad dressing instead
Cooked egg whites	becomes tough and rubbery	uncooked egg white freezes well
Custard, cream fillings	becomes soggy; separates	
Egg white frosting	becomes foamy	substitute butter icing
Sour cream	becomes thin, watery	may be stirred into dips and spreads
Potato in soups, stews	may discolor, become mushy	add to recipe after thawing
Fried food	loses crispness	
Bread crumb toppings	become soggy	reheat, uncovered, to crisp
Crisp vegetables and fruit with a high water content, such as celery, melons, lettuce and tomatoes	lose crispness	use in cooked dishes, where texture is less important

General tips for freezing

• Make sure your freezer is maintaining at least 0° F (-18° C) or lower. Keep a thermometer in the freezer to check temperature.

• If you know you will be freezing a quantity of raw food, set the thermostat to the lowest setting prior to freezing, at least -10° F (-23° C); in fact, for any type of food, the faster it freezes the better.

• Freeze only small quantities of food at a time. As a rule, freeze no more than 2 to 3 lbs (1 to 1.5 kg) of food per cubic-foot capacity within a 24 hour period.

• Freeze in usable quantities suitable to the size of your family.

• Package food properly (see below).

• Clearly label each package with a description of the food, date frozen, serving size and type (for example, sliced or whole).

• Place food in the coldest part (back or bottom) of the freezer.

• Arrange packages to be frozen in a single layer with a little space between them so that air can circulate. Once frozen, packages can be moved close together and stacked.

Packaging for the freezer

For best quality, frozen foods must be packaged well. Poorly wrapped foods will lose moisture in the freezer, resulting in a condition commonly known as "freezer burn." This can be identified by discolored patches on the food which have a dried-out texture. Freezer burn does not affect food safety, but does affect its quality. Isolated patches of freezer burn can be cut away and discarded. But where it is extensive, the entire article may have to be discarded.

Here are some general rules about packaging for the freezer:

• Use only moisture/vapor-proof wrapping materials designed for the freezer.

• Square or rectangular containers (rather than round) make the best use of freezer space.

• Containers or wrapping materials should be clean.

• Packaging materials must be able to withstand freezing temperatures without cracking or breaking; if you use glass, be sure that is freezer-proof.

• Wrappers should cling to the food to exclude as much air as possible.

• Choose a container size appropriate to the quantity of food you wish to store; if it's too large, the food will be exposed to too much air.

• Chill food quickly and thoroughly in refrigerator before wrapping; this speeds up freezing and helps retain color, flavor and texture.

• Remove as much air as possible from the container, either by pressing it out by hand or sucking it out with a straw.

• Keep packages as thin and flat as possible

• Leave enough *headspace* – that is, the space between the packed food and closure – to allow for expansion when freezing; suggested amounts are shown below.

PACKAGING	HEADSPACE ALLOWANCE
Dry pack (see pages 24-25, 29)	1/2 inch (1 cm) for pint (500 mL)
Syrup, sugar and liquid packs (see pages 24-25)	1/2 inch (1 cm) for pint (500 mL) 1 inch (2 cm) for quart (1 L)
Wide-neck jars or cartons	3/4 inch (1.5 cm)
Narrow-necked jars (pint)	3/4 inch (1.5 cm) for pint (500 mL) 1 inch (2 cm) for quart (1 L)

WHAT TYPE OF PACKAGING TO USE

There are two basic types of packaging suitable for freezing: *rigid* (best for soups, stocks and stews) and *flexible* (best for fruit, vegetables and baked goods). Both types should be durable, moisture/vapor-proof, leakproof, able to withstand freezer temperatures, resistant to oil, grease or water, easy to seal and easy to mark. The packaging must also protect foods from absorbing unwanted flavors or odors.

Of the rigid types of packaging, the best are plastic containers, ice cube trays, and baking dishes suitable for baked goods and prepared foods. Avoid previously used non-waxed cardboard cartons.

Recommended flexible packaging includes wraps such as heavy aluminum foil, durable plastic films, laminated freezer papers, as well as sealable freezer bags. Not recommended are heavy freezer papers that are waxed only one side, butcher paper, waxed paper, stretch wrap or thin plastic bags.

Wrapping meat for the freezer

Meats can be packaged using either the "drugstore wrap" or "butcher wrap" methods (see diagram, page 14). It is safe to freeze meat or poultry in its supermarket wrapping for short-term storage (1 to 2 months). For longer storage, overwrap with a plastic bag, heavy foil, or place in airtight freezer containers.

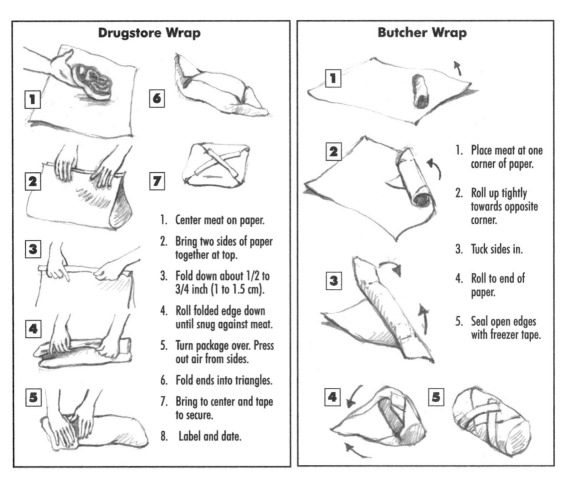

Drugstore Wrap

1. Center meat on paper.
2. Bring two sides of paper together at top.
3. Fold down about 1/2 to 3/4 inch (1 to 1.5 cm).
4. Roll folded edge down until snug against meat.
5. Turn package over. Press out air from sides.
6. Fold ends into triangles.
7. Bring to center and tape to secure.
8. Label and date.

Butcher Wrap

1. Place meat at one corner of paper.
2. Roll up tightly towards opposite corner.
3. Tuck sides in.
4. Roll to end of paper.
5. Seal open edges with freezer tape.

How long will it keep?

Food will not go bad while frozen but freezing too long will affect the quality of flavor, texture and nutritional value. No two foods freeze equally well. See chart below to see how long you can freeze different foods and still preserve their quality.

FREEZER STORAGE GUIDE

Maximum recommended storage times for foods properly packaged and frozen at 0° F (-18° C). Exceeding these times will not generally affect food safety but will affect the color, flavor and texture of food.

Fruits and Vegetables	1 year
Herbs	1 year
DAIRY PRODUCTS	
Butter, salted	1 year
Butter, unsalted	3 months
Cheese, processed (firm)	3 months

Cream, table, whipping		1 month (note: separates on thawing)
Milk		up to 6 weeks
Ice-cream, commercial		1 month
Ice-cream, homemade		up to 2 days
Margarine		6 months
Eggs, separated,	whites yolks mixed 1/2 tsp (2 mL) salt or sugar/yolks	3 months

FISH AND SHELLFISH, UNCOOKED

Fish (fatty, such as salmon, mackerel, lake trout)	2 months
Fish (lean, such as cod, haddock, pike)	6 months
Shellfish	2 to 4 months

MEAT AND POULTRY, UNCOOKED

Beef roasts or steaks	6 to 12 months
Beef, ground	3 months
Beef, stewing	3 to 6 months
Lamb	6 to 9 months
Pork roasts, chops	3 to 6 months
Pork, ground	2 months
Veal	6 to 9 months
Cured or smoked meat such as bacon	1 to 2 months
Sausages, wieners	2 to 3 months
Variety meats, giblets	3 to 4 months
Poultry, pieces	6 months
Poultry, whole	1 year
Duck or goose	3 months
Game, large	9 months
Game, small	1 to 2 months

COOKED FOODS	
Bean, lentil casseroles	3 to 6 months
Casseroles, meat pies	3 months
Poultry	1 to 3 months
Leftover cooked meat	2 months
Soups (stocks, cream)	4 months
BAKED GOODS	
Breads (yeast, baked or unbaked)	8 months
Cakes, cookies	4 months
Pastries, quick breads (baked)	8 months
Pastry crust, unbaked	2 months
Pie (fruit, unbaked)	6 months
Sandwiches	6 weeks

How to thaw frozen food

While proper packaging, temperature and storage times all affect the quality of frozen food, the method you use to thaw it is no less important. As you might expect, the correct thawing method varies with the type of food.

For example, **meat** should be thawed in the refrigerator (allow 1 day for each 5 lbs [2.5 kg]) or in the microwave or in a bath of cold water. If thawed in the microwave, the meat must be used immediately afterwards because cooking has already started. If using a water bath, check to see that the water stays cold.

Frozen **vegetables** can be cooked directly from frozen (except corn on the cob), but cooking times should be only one-half to two-thirds as long as fresh. Do not overcook.

Frozen **fruit** can be thawed partially at room temperature; it is best served with some ice crystals remaining. If the fruit is to be used in a cooked dish, it can be used directly from the freezer.

For baking, frozen unbaked goods (such as pastry or muffin batter) can go directly from freezer to oven. Thaw previously baked goods (such as bread or cakes), covered, at room temperature.

Casseroles can be thawed or partially thawed in the refrigerator, then reheated in the oven. If only partially thawed, allow up to 50% more heating time. As a rule, though, the quality of the food will be better if it is allowed to thaw slowly and completely in the refrigerator. Typically, a casserole will require 24 hours thawing time. Just be sure that you don't thaw the food at room temperature, which is ideal for rapid bacterial growth.

Keep in mind that, even when properly packaged and stored, some foods will change as a result of freezing and may require specific steps to correct these changes – either before freezing or after the food has been thawed. Some examples are given below:

- Gravies may thicken and need more broth added upon reheating.

- Sauces may separate and need to be whisked upon reheating.

- Vegetables, rice and pasta should be slightly undercooked for the freezer because they soften during the freezing process.

- Whipping (35%) cream can be frozen, but only if it is to be used in sauces, since it will not whip after freezing. However, whipped cream freezes.

- Seasonings such as onions, herbs and flavorings may change once they are frozen. You may need to alter the amount for freezing and add more seasoning on reheating. Pepper, cloves, garlic, green pepper, and imitation vanilla tend to get strong and bitter; celery seasonings become stronger, onion and paprika also change during freezing.

- Cheese changes in texture after being frozen. Hard cheeses become crumbly – which is still fine for cooking, but not slicing. Hard cheeses should frozen in 1-lb (500 g) blocks. Soft cheese, such as cream cheese, becomes watery and may need to be beaten or combined with other ingredients once thawed.

- Milk, yogurt and sour cream may separate to varying degrees when frozen; stir after thawing.

- Creamed cottage cheese separates and becomes mushy after freezing; stir after thawing.

- Whole egg (without sugar or salt) becomes gummy.

What type of freezer do you need?

A freezer is a 20-year investment, so you need to consider the type of freezer that best meets your needs. There are three basic types of freezers, each providing different combinations of features and benefits.

Chest freezers. These are the most affordable to purchase. They are also the most economical to operate, since little cold air escapes when the door is opened. However, a chest freezer requires the most floor space and is more awkward for organizing its contents; if you buy one, make sure that it is equipped with baskets for easy placement and removal of food. Generally, to decide on the size of the freezer you will require, allow 5 to 6 cubic feet per person. Remember, too, it is more energy-efficient to have a smaller freezer that is full than to have a larger one that is only partially filled.

Upright freezers. Refrigerator-like in design, upright freezers have one or two doors and anywhere from 3 to 7 shelves inside, making them much easier to organize than a chest freezer. Another advantage is that they take up little floor space. However, they are more expensive to operate since cold air escapes each time the door is opened.

Combination refrigerator-freezers. This is the type that just about everyone has, since most refrigerators have a freezer built in. Depending on the model, the freezer may be just a compartment within the refrigerator, or it may be a separate section with its own door; the latter type is more efficient to operate since it is not opened and closed as often. Check to make sure the freezer can maintain a temperature of 0° F (-18° C) or lower. The disadvantage of this type of freezer is that it lacks the space of a stand-alone model. But for a small family, it may be perfectly adequate.

Caring for your freezer

Freezers (of any type) should be placed in a cool, dry, well ventilated place, away from potential sources of heat, such as the sun, a water heater or stove.

DEFROSTING

For efficient operation and to maintain proper temperatures, manual-defrost freezers need to be defrosted at least once a year or when there is more than 1/2 inch (1 cm) frost on the walls. Disconnect the freezer and follow the manufacturer's instructions for defrosting. If possible, plan to defrost your freezer when it contains the least amount of food. While defrosting, frozen food can be stored in insulated ice chests or wrapped in several layers of newspapers and stored in cardboard cartons. Place towels in the bottom of the freezer to catch any frost or water. Loose frost can be removed with wooden or plastic scrapers.

Once the frost is removed, wipe out the freezer with a solution of 1 tbsp (15 mL) baking soda per 4 cups (1 L) water. Dry well. Turn the freezer on and close the door, allowing approximately 20 minutes for the freezer to cool down before returning food to the freezer. If food has frost on the outside, mark these packages and use them first.

Frost-free freezers do not need to be defrosted, but they do need to be emptied and cleaned once a year in the same way as described above.

RE-FREEZING FOODS

If frozen foods have thawed but still have ice crystals present, they may be refrozen as quickly as possible in the coldest part of the freezer. If food has thawed completely and has been exposed to temperatures above 50° F (10° C) for several hours, discard vegetables and processed meats. Fruits may be cooked and used, as can poultry and other meats – providing they have a fresh smell. If in doubt, discard the food.

REMOVING ODORS

If food has spoiled in the freezer, it can leave unpleasant odors. These can be removed by taking the food from the freezer and washing the freezer with a solution of 1 tbsp (15 mL) baking soda per 4 cups (1 L) water or 1 cup (250 mL) vinegar to 16 cups (4 L) water. Allow freezer to dry.

If odor is still present, purchase a container of activated charcoal (available at drugstores or pet stores) and place pans of this in the bottom of the freezer for several days. If the odor is still there, remove old charcoal and replace with new. Repeat process. When the odor has gone, rinse and dry the freezer.

If the odor has penetrated the insulation of the freezer, contact the freezer manufacturer for suggestions. There may be nothing that can be done.

FREEZER EMERGENCIES

If your freezer stops working, first check the fuses before calling the repairman. Frozen food will stay frozen for 2 to 3 days, providing the freezer door is kept closed. Usually, this is long enough to have the freezer repaired. If not, remove the food to insulated ice chests (or to another freezer, if available) until your freezer is working.

Organizing your freezer

While freezing is a relatively simple process, it can be a real challenge to keep track of what food is stored, where it is stored and when it was stored in the freezer. For this reason, a food inventory is essential. Here are some tips for successfully organizing your freezer.

• Group similar types of foods together so you keep track of what you have on hand and can more easily find the food you want. Use baskets in a chest freezer.

• Label all foods clearly with what it is, the date on which it was frozen, how it was frozen (whether, for instance, it is whole or sliced), as well as the serving size.

• As you add new food, bring the older food to the front (or top) so that it will be used next.

• Keep a list taped to the front (or top) of the freezer showing what is inside with the date it went into the freezer. Cross off items as they are removed from the freezer.

• Be ruthless! Get rid of any mystery food you cannot identify or anything that is beyond the "best before" date. (See storage guide, pages 14 to 16.)

• To use space most efficiently, store food in square containers and/or as flat as possible.

• Use clear plastic containers (where appropriate) to let you see what is inside.

freezing fresh foods

One of the greatest benefits of a freezer is that it allows you to preserve seasonal fruits and vegetables when they are at their best so you can enjoy high-quality, nutritious produce at any time of the year. If you have a large garden, freezing is a natural for preserving your end-of-summer bounty. But even apartment dwellers can benefit from freezing fruits and vegetables that are available in season at markets and pick-your-own farms.

Freezing is also a an excellent way to preserve fresh meats, allowing you to buy in quantity and take advantage of the best prices.

Preserving your harvest

In this chapter, we'll look at the specific techniques that you can use for freezing different types of foods. Let's start with some general rules for ensuring that your frozen fruits and vegetables keep their "garden fresh" taste:

• Freeze as quickly after harvesting as possible because fruits and vegetables continue to undergo chemical changes that can cause spoilage and deterioration.

• Select only the best quality fruit and vegetables. Freezing will not improve the quality of produce.

• Freeze fruit with ascorbic acid to deactivate enzymes (see chart, pages 26 to 27).

• Blanching vegetables is essential to inactivate enzymes and produce a top quality product. (see chart, pages 30 to 34).

• Store frozen fruits and vegetables at 0° F (-18° C) or lower, and use with 1 year.

DEACTIVATING ENZYMES

All fruits and vegetables contain enzymes that help them ripen. This is essential to their proper development, of course, but somewhat inconvenient after the produce has been harvested, since the ripening process continues and can cause food spoilage if the enzymes are not deactivated.

To deactivate enzymes in vegetables, the produce must be *blanched* – that is, exposed to boiling water for a required period of time, then rapidly chilled in ice water. This process helps destroy micro-organisms on the surface of the vegetable, brightens the color, retards loss of vitamins and helps make some bulky vegetables (like broccoli and cauliflower) more compact.

Enzymes in fruits produce browning and loss of vitamin C. Instead of blanching, as with vegetables, the enzyme action is controlled by coating the fruit in ascorbic acid (available in drugstores or, under the commercial name of Fruitfresh, in supermarkets).

Taking out the air

One of the main causes of rancid flavor in fruits and vegetables is when the frozen produce comes into contact with air. To prevent this problem, it is important to wrap the produce tightly, pressing out as much air as possible. Any remaining air should be removed by sucking it out with a straw from the freezer bag prior to freezing.

What affects texture

Frozen fruit and vegetables, once thawed, are softer than fresh because the process of freezing causes water within the cell walls to expand and rupture the membrane. High-starch vegetables, like corn and peas, contain less water; thus, their texture is also less likely to change. Another factor is the speed with which the produce is frozen: the faster it freezes, the smaller the ice crystals formed within the cells, which minimizes cell rupture. Therefore, for the best texture, it is important to set the freezer at the lowest setting several hours prior to freezing and only freeze 2 to 3 lbs (1 to 1.5 kg) of produce per cubic foot of freezer in a 24-hour period.

How to freeze fruit

You can capture that "just picked flavor" in fruits with very little effort. The simplest method is unsweetened pack – that is, to freeze individual fruits (like berries) on a baking sheet lined with waxed paper then pack in usable amounts (usually 2 or 4 cups [500 mL or 1 L]) in freezer bags. Voila! Summer in a bag – a real treat in mid-winter.

Freezing fruit typically involves one of the following methods:

Unsweetened pack. Fruit is frozen individually on a tray then packed into freezer bags. This simple method is suitable for cherries, strawberries, red and black currants, blackberries, blueberries, gooseberries, cranberries, raspberries and chopped rhubarb. The fruit can be used in jams, jellies, desserts and sugar-restricted diets.

Syrup pack. Fruits are frozen in a syrup – either heavy, medium, thin or very thin (the latter two types may also be called "light") – and stored in a container. This is best for uncooked desserts such as fruit salads.

Dry pack. Fruits are coated in sugar with ascorbic acid (for apples, peaches and apricots) and frozen. This is best for desserts that will be cooked, such as pies.

Try these steps to success.

1. Prepare your equipment. Assemble all necessary equipment and make sure it is clean. Do not use iron or copper equipment that can react with the acid in fruit. Earthenware, glass or stainless steel utensils are considered safe.

2. Sort fruit and remove damaged, overripe or underripe pieces. Wash fruit gently, lifting it out of the water to leave dirt in sink or bowl. Do not allow fruit to soak in water. Do not wash blueberries before freezing, since it makes the skin tough. Do not wash raspberries, which are too fragile.

3. Prepare the fruit according to packing method chosen:

   Unsweetened pack: Simply spread a single layer of prepared fruit on shallow tray lined with waxed paper and freeze. This method is suitable for strawberries, blueberries, blackberries, cherries, raspberries, gooseberries, cranberries, currants and rhubarb. Do not wash raspberries or blueberries prior to freezing. Because accurate measurements are important for jam making, measure fruit prior to packing in freezer bags and mark on bags.

   Syrup pack. Make sugar syrup depending on the tartness of the fruit and according to personal taste. For 1 quart (1 L) syrup you will add 1/4 tsp (1 mL) powder or crystal ascorbic acid, or 750 mg in tablet form. If using tablets, dissolve in 1 tbsp (15 mL) water first before adding to syrup.

TYPE OF SYRUP	SUGAR	WATER	YIELD
Very thin	1 cup (250 mL)	2 cups (500 mL)	about 2 1/2 cups (625 mL)
Thin	1 cup (250 mL)	1 1/2 cups (375 mL)	about 2 cups (500 mL)
Medium	1 cup (250 mL)	1 cup (250 mL)	about 1 1/2 cups (375 mL)
Heavy	1 cup (250 mL)	3/4 cup (175 mL)	about 1 1/4 cups (300 mL)

   Dry pack. Mix fruit and measured amount of sugar (see chart) in bowl; stir gently.

5. Deactivate enzymes. Fruits like apples, peaches, plums, nectarines and sweet cherries will darken once surfaces are exposed to air. Add 1/4 tsp (1 mL) of powdered or crystal ascorbic acid to each quart (1 L) of fruit or 750 mg of tablet form dissolved in 1 tablespoon (15 mL) water to prevent darkening. For a commercial variety of ascorbic acid such as Fruitfresh, use directions on package. If you are freezing unsweetened packs of fruits that will darken, be sure to have powdered ascorbic acid to sprinkle on fruit before freezing.

6. Pack in plastic freezer bags, freezer containers or freezer jars with straight sides. Allow required headspace for expansion. See chart below.

HEADSPACE REQUIRED FOR WIDE-TOP CONTAINERS

PACKING TYPE	1-PINT (500 mL) SIZE	1-QUART (1 L) SIZE
Liquid	1/2 inch (1 cm)	1 inch (2 cm)
Dry	1/2 inch (1 cm)	1/2 inch (1 cm)

HEADSPACE REQUIRED FOR NARROW-TOP CONTAINERS

PACKING TYPE	1-PINT (500 mL) SIZE	1-QUART (1 L) SIZE
Liquid	3/4 inch (1 cm)	1 1/2 inches (3.5 cm)
Dry	1/2 inch (1 cm)	1/2 inch (1 cm)

FREEZING TIPS FOR SPECIFIC FRUITS

APPLES

Choose firm, crisp, well-flavored apples. Wash, peel, core and slice. Hold in weak brine (2 tsp [10 mL] salt to 1 qt [1 L] water) to prevent discoloration while slicing. Drain before packing. **Note:** *Apple slices blanched in a large quantity of boiling water for 1 to 2 minutes, depending on variety and maturity, do not discolor readily; however, there is some loss in flavor. Pack in dry sugar (1 cup [250 mL] sugar to 4 cups [1 L] prepared fruit). Ascorbic acid may be added.* Prepare applesauce with favorite recipe. Cool and pack, leaving sufficient headspace. See freezer pie filling.

APRICOTS

Choose firm, ripe fruit with no green shoulders. Wash, halve and pit. Do not blanch. For pies, wash, quarter and pit.
Note: *Quality is only fair. Pack in cold syrup (2 cups [500 mL] sugar to 3 cups [750 mL] water). Leave headspace.*
Pack in dry sugar using 2/3 cup (150 mL) sugar to 4 cups (l L) prepared fruit. Ascorbic acid may be added to either pack.

BANANAS

Freeze whole with skin on. Thaw at room temperature. Peel. Mash. Flesh suitable for baking, milkshakes.

BLACKBERRIES

Choose plump, sweet, firm, ripe berries. Sort for maturity and wash. Freeze without sugar on waxed paper lined trays. Store in freezer bags.

BLUEBERRIES

Choose sweet, well-ripened berries; do not wash, since washing toughens skin. Instead, wash just before using. Freeze without sugar, on waxed paper-lined trays; once frozen, freeze in freezer bags.

CANTALOUPE

See Melons

CHERRIES, SOUR

Choose firm, ripe cherries. Wash, stem and pit. Pack in dry sugar using 1 cup (250 mL) sugar to 4 cups (1 L) prepared fruit. Freeze in freezer bags or rigid plastic containers.

CHERRIES, SWEET

Only fair quality. Choose tree-ripened, firm, sweet cherries. Black varieties are preferred. Sort, stem, wash and pit (if desired). Unpitted: freeze without sugar or pack in cold syrup. (2 cups [500 mL] sugar to 3 cups [750 mL] water). Leave 1 inch (2 cm) headspace. Pitted: Pack in dry sugar, using 1/2 cup (125 mL) sugar to 4 cups (l L) prepared fruit. Addition of ascorbic acid improves color and flavor.

CRANBERRIES

Choose deep red, uniform-colored, firm, glossy-skinned berries. Wash and stem or freeze in freezer bags as bought from supermarket. Freeze without sugar on waxed paper-lined trays. Once frozen, store in freezer bags.

CURRANTS, RED AND BLACK

Choose well-ripened currants. Wash and stem. Freeze without sugar on waxed paper-lined trays. Once frozen, store in freezer bags.

GOOSEBERRIES

Choose fully mature berries. Sort, wash, remove stems and blossom ends. Freeze without sugar on waxed paper-lined trays. Once frozen, store in freezer bags.

GRAPES

Wash carefully to remove spray deposits. Detach from stems. Freeze without sugar on waxed paper-lined trays. Once frozen, store in freezer bags. Suitable for use in jam, jelly or juice.

MELON, CANTALOUPE, MUSKMELON

Choose fully-ripened, firm, well-colored melons. Wash, cut in half, remove seeds and zest. Cut into cubes, slices or balls. Pack in cold syrup (1 cup [250 mL] sugar to 2 1/2 cups [625 mL] water). Leave headspace as in chart, page 25.

PEARS

Not recommended for freezing.

PEACHES

Choose firm, ripe peaches with no green color in the skin. Peel, pit and slice. Select varieties that do not brown readily, such as Redhaven, Envoy, Harmony, Madison, Veteran, Sunbeam. Pack in cold syrup (2 cups [500 mL] sugar to 3 cups [750mL] water). Pack in dry sugar using 2/3 cup (150 mL) sugar to 4 cups (1 L) prepared fruit. Ascorbic acid may be added to either pack.

PLUMS

Choose firm, mature fruit. Sort, wash, halve and pit. **Note**: *Quality is only fair.* Pack in cold syrup (2 cups [500mL] sugar to 3 cups [750mL] water). Leave headspace. Pack in dry sugar using 3/4 cup sugar to 4 cups prepared fruit. Ascorbic acid may be added to any pack.

RASPBERRIES

Choose firm, fully mature fruit. Try not to wash. Freeze without sugar on waxed paper-lined trays. Pack into freezer bags.

RHUBARB

Choose tender, well-colored stalks. Wash, trim, cut into 1-inch lengths. Freeze without sugar on waxed paper-lined trays. Pack into freezer bags.

STRAWBERRIES

Choose firm, fully ripe, red, vine-ripened berries. Sort, wash in cold water and hull. Do not soak. Slicing improves texture and flavor. Freeze without sugar on waxed paper-lined trays; pack into freezer bags.
Dry pack: mix 4 cups (1 L) berries with 2/3 cup (150 mL) granulated sugar.

Thawing frozen fruit

Frozen fruit is best served with a few ice crystals left. If fruit is going to be cooked, thaw only enough to separate fruit and cook from frozen or thaw at room temperature to serve as fresh fruit such as fruit salad with a few ice crystals still in fruit.

How to freeze vegetables

Although most vegetables can be frozen, they often lose their original texture in the process and, once thawed, cannot be used as fresh. However, they can be used in stews, soups and casseroles very success-fully. Vegetables are subject to enzyme action. So, with a few exceptions – notably rutabagas, leeks, bell peppers and herbs – they must be blanched (immersed for a short time in boiling water) before freezing.

Try these steps to success.

1. Prepare your equipment the night before so that once the vegeta-bles are picked or purchased fresh from a market you can immedi-ately start to process them. You will need:

   • Large pot, with a minimum 2-gallon (9 L) capacity

   • Colander, net bag, cheesecloth or wire basket for blanching

   • Large pans of cold water for cooling

   • Ice cubes or ice blocks for cooling

   • Cutting boards, knives, hot pads

   • Plastic freezer bags or other suitable freezer containers

   • A kitchen timer or clock with a second hand

2. Choose vegetables at their peak – freezing will not improve quality. Vegetables start to deteriorate hours after they are picked, so the sooner they are processed the better. If possible, plan to pick in the cool of the morning. If you are unable to prepare vegetables imme-diately for freezing, keep them in the refrigerator at a temperature of not more than 40° F (4° C) – preferably 32° F (0° C) – to main-tain quality and nutrients.

3. Blanch the vegetables. In the large pot, bring 1 gallon of water to a boil (2 gallons if blanching leafy vegetables). Place no more than a 1 lb (500 g) of the vegetables on a large square of cheesecloth or in a wire basket and lower it into the boiling water. Shake the vegeta-bles slightly to spread out (this ensures even heating). Cover the

pot and wait until the water returns to a boil. Then start counting the recommended blanching time (see chart on pages 30 to 34). Be sure to time the blanching carefully: too little time and the enzymes will not be deactivated; too much time will destroy nutrients and result in loss of color and flavor. Microwaves are not recommended for blanching.

Blanching water may be used several times, although you may need to add more to compensate for evaporation and keep the total volume of water constant. Once the water becomes cloudy, it must be changed. Keep in mind that the quality of water you use for blanching can affect the texture of some vegetables. For example, hard water (that which has a high mineral content) can cause green beans to toughen.

4. After the required blanching time, remove the vegetable from the pot and immediately cool them under cold running water (or in pans of ice water). The cooling time should be about the same as blanching time. Drain the vegetables thoroughly to minimize the formation of ice crystals during freezing.

5. Pack using one of the methods described below. Use odorless, tasteless, airtight, moisture-proof containers such as freezer bags with ties, rigid containers with a snap lid, straight-sided jars with screw top, or heavily waxed cardboard cartons.

    Dry pack. Place the vegetables into a plastic container and pack tightly to cut down on the amount of air in the container. Leave 1/2 inch (1 cm) headspace and seal container with lid. Or, if using freezer bags, press out as much air as you can or suck it out with a straw, tightly twist the bag and seal with a tie.

    Tray pack. As the name suggests, this method involves freezing vegetables on a tray before packing them into a freezer bag or plastic container. It produces a product similar to commercially frozen vegetables, and is especially good for peas, corn and beans. Arrange blanched vegetables on the tray and place in freezer just until they are frozen, then pack into a bag or container. Do not leave headspace. Seal tightly.

6. Freeze at 0° F (-18° C) or lower. Properly prepared, good-quality vegetables should keep well for at least 1 year and for as long as 1 1/2 years.

FREEZING TIPS FOR SPECIFIC VEGETABLES

ARTICHOKE, GLOBE

Preparation: Select small artichokes or hearts. Remove outer leaves; cut off top of bud; trim stem; wash thoroughly.

Blanching: Blanch in citric acid solution or ascorbic acid (1 tbsp [15 mL] citric acid crystals or 1/2 cup [125 mL] lemon juice or 1/2 tbsp [7 mL] ascorbic acid in 8 cups [2 L] water). Blanch small hearts, 3 minutes; large hearts, 5 minutes; small whole artichokes, 10 minutes. Cool in cold water 5 to 10 minutes.

Packing: Drain well, package and freeze at once in freezer bags.

ASPARAGUS

Preparation: Loses quality quickly after harvest. Chill or process immediately. Select young, tender stalks with compact tips. Wash thoroughly in cold water. If there is sand under leaflets, soak and wash in warm water or remove leaflets. Grade stalks into small (up to 1/4 inch [5 mm] diameter); medium (1/4 to 1/2 inch [5 mm to 1 cm] diameter); and large (over 1/2 inch [1 cm] diameter). Leftover ends can be blanched, packaged, frozen and used for soup. Small stalks may be slightly stringy. Frozen asparagus can have a poor texture; purée for soups and sauces.

Blanching: small, 2 minutes; medium, 3 minutes; large, 4 minutes. Chill quickly in cold water.

Packing: Drain and package spears alternating tip and stem ends. Freeze at one in freezer bags.

BEANS, GREEN AND WAX

Preparation: Select young, tender, stringless beans. Wash thoroughly, remove ends (and strings if any). Leave whole, cut or break into 1-inch (2 cm) pieces or cut lengthwise for julienne style. Flavor may be weak after freezing.

Blanching: cut, 2 to 3 minutes; whole, 3 to 4 minutes; julienne, 2 to 3 minutes

Packing: Drain, package and freeze at once in freezer bags.

BEANS, LIMA

Preparation: Select well-filled pods. Beans should be green but not starchy or mealy. Wash pods and remove beans or blanch pods and beans together for easier removal of beans.

Blanching: small, 2 minutes; medium, 3 minutes; large, 4 minutes. Add 1 minute if beans are blanched in pod. Chill quickly in cold water and remove beans from pods.

Packing: Drain, package and freeze at once in freezer bags.

BEETS

Preparation: Select young, tender beets up to 2 inches (5 cm) in diameter (avoid woody beets). Trim, leaving 1/2-inch (1 cm) stem, wash and sort as to small or medium size. Remove skin after cooking.

Blanching: small, 25 to 30 minutes; medium, 35 to 40 minutes. Cook until ready to eat. Chill in cold water.

Packing: Leave whole, slice or dice after cooking. Package and freeze at once in freezer bags.

BEET GREENS

See Greens

BROCCOLI

Preparation: Select dark green, compact heads with sound, tender stalks. If necessary, soak in salt solution for half an hour to loosen insects and then rinse 6 tbsp (90 mL) salt per gallon (4 L) cold water. Separate heads into pieces not thicker than 1 inch (2 cm). Split large stems lengthwise.

Blanching: small to medium, 3 minutes; large, 4 minutes. Chill quickly in cold water.

Packing: Drain and package. Freeze at once in freezer bags.

BRUSSELS SPROUTS

Preparation: Select dark green sprouts with firm, compact heads. Wash, trim off coarse outer leaves and inspect carefully for insects. Sort sprouts into small, medium and large if there is much variation in size.

Blanching: small, 3 to 4 minutes; medium, 4 minutes; large, 5 minutes. Chill quickly in cold water.

Packing: Drain and package. Freeze at once in freezer bags.

CABBAGE

Preparation: Select solid heads. Trim off coarse outer leaves. Shred, cut into wedges or separate individual leaves for cabbage rolls. *Note: Use only for cooking.*

Blanching: Shredded or leaves, 1 to 1/2 minutes; wedges, 2 to 3 minutes. Chill quickly in cold water. Individual leaves for cabbage rolls.

Packing: Drain and package. Freeze at once in freezer bags.

CARROTS

Preparation: Select young, tender carrots. Remove tops, wash thoroughly, scrape or peel. Small carrots can be left whole. Dice or slice larger carrots into pieces 1/4 inch (5 mm) thick or cut lengthwise into strips.

Blanching: whole, 4 to 5 minutes; diced: 3 minutes; sliced, 3 minutes; strips, 3 minutes. Chill quickly in cold water.

Packing: Drain and package. Freeze at once in freezer bags.

CAULIFLOWER

Preparation: Select firm, compact, snow-white heads. Trim and cut into serving pieces – about 1 inch (2 cm) thick. Wash thoroughly and if necessary soak in a salt solution (6 tbsp [90 mL] salt per gallon [4 L] water) for 30 minutes to remove insects, then rinse.

Blanching: 4 minutes. Chill quickly in cold water.

Packing: Drain and package. Freeze at once in freezer bags.

CELERY

Preparation: Select stalks which are crisp and tender, free from coarse strings and pithiness. Wash thoroughly and cut into desired lengths for soups or other dishes to be cooked.

Blanching: 3 minutes. Chill quickly in cold water.

Packing: Drain and package in small lots. Freeze at once in freezer bags.

CHIVES

See Herbs

COLLARDS

See Greens

CORN, CUT (WHOLE KERNEL OR CREAM STYLE)

Preparation: Select ears ready for table use. Remove husk and silk. Discard immature ears (undersized kernels with watery milk), and overmature ears (relatively tough kernels with thick milk). Wash, cut kernels from cob after blanching. For whole kernel, cut from cob at 2/3 depth of kernel; for cream style, cut from cob at 1/2 depth of kernel. Reverse knife and scrape cob to remove juice and hearts of kernels.

Blanching: 4 minutes. Chill quickly in cold water.

Packing: Drain, cut kernels from cob and freeze at once in freezer bags.

CORN, ON THE COB

Preparation: Select ears as for cut corn. Trim ends and sort cobs into small, medium and large. Wash thoroughly. Blanching: small, 7 minutes; medium, 9 minutes; large, 11 minutes. Chill quickly in cold water.

Packing: Drain and package. Freeze at once in freezer bags.

DANDELION GREENS

See Greens

FREEZING TIPS FOR SPECIFIC VEGETABLES

EGGPLANT

Preparation: Select fruit with soft seeds. Peel and cut into slices 1/2 inch (1 cm) thick. Blanch in citric or ascorbic acid (2 tsp [10 mL] citric acid crystals or 2 tbsp [25 mL] lemon juice or 1 tsp [5 mL] ascorbic acid in 8 cups [2 L] water).

Blanching: 2 minutes. Chill quickly in cold water. Slices will darken during blanching.

Packing: Drain and package. Freeze at once in freezer bags.

FIDDLEHEADS

See Greens

GRAPE LEAVES

See Greens

GREENS (BEET, DANDELION, MUSTARD, TURNIP; COLLARDS, FIDDLEHEADS, GRAPE LEAVES, KALE, SPINACH, SWISS CHARD)

Preparation: Select young, tender leaves. Wash well. Discard imperfect leaves and tough stems. Agitate during blanching and cooling, to stop leaves from matting.

Blanching: grape leaves, 1 1/2 minutes; beet, kale, mustard, turnip, 1 or 2 minutes; collards, dandelion, fiddleheads, spinach, Swiss chard, 3 minutes. All greens: Chill quickly in cold water.

Packing: Drain and package at once in freezer bags.

HERBS SUCH AS BASIL, DILL, MARJORAM, MINT, PARSLEY, ROSEMARY, SAGE, TARRAGON, CHIVES, THYME, AND OREGANO.

Preparation: Wash, dry and chop. Wrap in plastic, wrap in individual packages; label and put together in large package.

Blanching: Not necessary. If in a rush, leave leaves whole. Freeze on trays. Pack in freezer bags.

Packing: Ready to use in recipes.

KALE

See Greens

KOHLRABI

Preparation: Select young, tender, medium-sized heads. Cut off tops and roots. Wash. Peel. Leave whole or dice into 1/2-inch (1 cm) cubes.

Blanching: whole, 4 to 5 minutes; cubes, 2 to 3 minutes. Chill quickly in cold water.

Packing: Drain and package. Freeze at once.

LEEKS

Preparation: Wash. Chop into small pieces. Use in soups, casseroles and stews.

Blanching: Not necessary.

Packing: Package small amounts in tightly sealed containers or freezer bags.

MUSHROOMS

Preparation: Select mushrooms free from spots. They can be blanched or sautéed. For blanching, wash thoroughly and trim off ends of stems. If larger than 1 inch (2 cm) in diameter, slice or cut in quarters. Blanch in a weak solution of ascorbic or citric acid (1 tsp [5 mL] citric acid or 1 tbsp [15 mL] lemon juice or 1/2 tsp [2 mL] ascorbic acid powder to 2 cups [500 mL] water). To sauté, wash lightly to remove grit from surface. Large mushrooms should be sliced. Sauté small amounts at a time in butter or oil for 1 minute; cool cooked mushrooms In a bowl placed in cold water.

Blanching: slices, 2 to 3 minutes; small whole mushrooms and quarters, 3 to 4 minutes; large, 4 to 5 minutes. Chill quickly in cold water.

Packing: Drain and package. Freeze at once in freezer bags.

MUSTARD GREENS

See Greens

BROCCOLI AND CHEESE-STUFFED POTATOES (PAGE 50) ➤

FREEZING TIPS FOR SPECIFIC VEGETABLES

OKRA

Preparation: Select young, tender, green pods. Wash thoroughly. Remove stems but do not open pod. Sort into small and large, if necessary. Slice, if desired, after blanching. Use in soups or stews.

Blanching: small pods, 3 minutes; large pods, 4 minutes. Chill quickly in cold water.

Packing: Drain and package. Freeze at once in freezer bags.

ONION

Preparation: Chop and freeze for stews and soups. *Note: While onions can be frozen, this is not usually necessary because they keep well in a cool, dry place. They tend to lose flavor after 3 to 6 months.* Select mature, good quality onions. Sweet Spanish types are preferred but any good garden variety will do. Peel, wash, slice in rings or chop. Chopped or sliced best used in cooking.

Blanching: 1 1/2 minutes Chill quickly in cold water.

Packing: Drain and package, in tightly sealed containers. Freeze at once in freezer bags.

PARSNIPS

Preparation: Select small- to medium-sized parsnips, free from woodiness. Wash thoroughly and peel. Dice into 1/2-inch (1 cm) cubes or slices.

Blanching: 2 minutes. Chill quickly in cold water.

Packing: Drain and package. Freeze at once in freezer bags.

PEAS

Preparation: Process soon after harvest, since peas lose quality quickly. Select plump, firm pods. Do not use immature or tough peas. Shell before blanching. Leave snowpeas whole.

Blanching: 2 minutes. Chill quickly in cold water 1 1/2 minutes.

Packing: Drain and package. Freeze at once in freezer bags.

PEPPERS, BELL OR SWEET (RED, YELLOW, GREEN, ORANGE)

Preparation: Select firm, crisp, thick-walled, green, red or yellow. Wash and remove seeds, pulp and stem. Can be frozen in halves, cut into strips or slices, or diced. Use unblanched peppers in uncooked foods; blanched peppers for cooking.

Blanching: Not required, but can be put in boiling water for 2 to 3 minutes to facilitate packaging.

Packing: Pack in tightly sealed containers; peppers can impart odors to the freezer.

PEPPERS, HOT

Preparation: Wash and stem peppers.

Blanching: Not required.

Packing: Pack in small containers, seal and freeze in freezer bags.

POTATOES, FRENCH FRIED

Preparation: Select mature potatoes. Wash, peel and cut into 1/2-inch (1 cm) sticks. Cook in oil until light brown. Do not cook completely. Remove from oil to cool. To serve, reheat on a greased baking sheet at 450° F (230° C) for 10 to 15 minutes, turning once.

Blanching: n/a. Cook until almost done.

Packing: Drain and package. Freeze at once.

POTATOES, MASHED

Preparation: Select any good quality potato. Wash, peel and cook completely. Drain and mash with butter, milk and seasonings. See Much More Mash (recipe, page 116).

Blanching: n/a. Cook completely.

Packing: Package, leaving 1/2 inch (1 cm) headspace. Freeze at once.

≺ VEGGIE BEEF AND PASTA BAKE (PAGE 53)

FREEZING TIPS FOR SPECIFIC VEGETABLES

POTATOES, SWEET

Preparation: Select mature potatoes. If freshly dug, allow to cure 10 to 15 days at 80° F (25° C). Wash and sort into sizes. Cook until almost tender. Peel. Leave whole, cut in halves, slice or mash. To stop prepared sweet potatoes from darkening, dip whole, halves or slices in a critic acid solution for 5 sec (1 tbsp [15 mL] citric acid crystals or 1/2 cup (125 mL) lemon juice in 4 cups [1 L] water). For mashed sweet potatoes, add 2 tbsp (15 mL) orange or lemon juice per 4 cups (1 L) potato; stir in well.
Blanching: n/a. Cook completely.
Packing: Package, leaving 1/2 inch (1 cm) headspace. Freeze at once.

PUMPKIN

See Squash

RUTABAGAS

Preparation: Select sound rutabagas. Wash, peel and dice into 1/2 inch (1 cm) cubes.
Blanching: Not required.
Packing: Package and freeze at once in freezer bags.

SPINACH

See Greens

SQUASH, SUMMER (ZUCCHINI)

Preparation: Select young squash with small seeds and tender zest. Wash, cut in 1/2 inch (1 cm) slices. Use for soups.
Blanching: 3 minutes. Chill quickly in cold water.
Packing: Drain and package. Freeze at once in freezer bags.

SQUASH, WINTER (PUMPKIN)

Preparation: Select well-matured squash or pumpkin. Wash, cut in half and remove seeds and connective tissue. Peel, bake halves until tender. Peel, cut into even cubes, boil or steam until tender; may be puréed in food processor.
Blanching: Bake at 350° F (180° C) for 40 to 60 minutes. Boil 15 to 20 minutes. Steam 30 to 60 minutes Cool in refrigerator.
Packing: Package leaving 1/2 inch (1 cm) headspace. Freeze at once in freezer bags.

SWISS CHARD

See Greens

TOMATO, JUICE

Preparation: Select firm, vine-ripened tomatoes. Wash and trim. Cut in quarters or eighths. Simmer 5 minutes. Strain through fine sieve.
Blanching: Simmer 5 minutes; add 1 tsp (5 mL) salt per 4 cups (1 L) juice. Cool in refrigerator.
Packing: Package in plastic container or glass jar, leaving 1 1/2-inch (3.5 cm) headspace; if in bottles, leave 2 to 3 inches (5 to 7.5 cm).

TOMATO, WHOLE

Preparation: For fast freeze, wash and freeze tomatoes whole on baking sheet. Pack in freezer bags and use in soups and stews. Or select fully ripened fruit. Wash and scald to loosen skin. Cool in cold water. Peel and core. Freeze as is or stew, adding 1 tsp (5 mL) salt per 1 qt (1 L). Tomatoes tend to be tough and stringy if not stewed before freezing. Use as a side plate or in cooked dishes. Once frozen they cannot be used as fresh.
Blanching: Scald 1 to 2 minutes to aid removal of skin. Stew 2 to 3 minutes.
Packing: Package in plastic containers or glass jar, leaving 1 1/2 inches (3.5 cm) headspace.

TURNIP GREENS

See Greens

Cooking frozen vegetables

With the exception of corn on the cob, frozen vegetables cook well without being thawed. Just thaw enough to remove them from their packaging and cook in a small amount of boiling water. Do not over-cook. The vegetable requires only one-half to two-thirds the cooking time needed for fresh vegetables.

Corn on the cob should be almost completely thawed before cooking or it will not heat through.

Do not refreeze vegetables after thawing. Quality suffers and there is always the chance of food spoilage.

How to freeze meat

As a rule, fresh meat freezes well. Here are some tips to ensure that nutrients, flavor and texture are preserved.

• **Quality**. Use only the best quality meat from a reliable dealer. This is particularly important if you buy and freeze in volume – for example, a whole side of beef or pork, or a carcass of lamb. Check that there is not too much fat on the carcass. It may be more economical to buy meat cuts on sale than to purchase a whole carcass.

• **Handling**. Be sure that fresh meat has been properly handled, under completely sanitary conditions. If you have any doubt, the meat should be cooked before freezing.

• **Packaging**. Wrap meat using either the "drugstore" or "butcher" method (see page 14 for technique) before freezing. Boneless cuts should first be trimmed of excess fat.

• **Labelling**. Each package should be labeled to indicate the cut, weight, number of servings and the date of freezing. Remember to list this on the inventory list on the outside of your freezer.

• **Fast freezing**. Meat should be frozen as quickly as possible. The best way is to have it frozen commercially at -10° F (-23° C) before taking it home to your freezer. Never freeze large quantities in a home freezer. Frozen meat should be stored at 0° F (-18° C). Storage times will vary depending on the type and method of processing (see chart, pages 14 to 15).

Thawing frozen meat

The best way is to thaw meat is in the refrigerator, where slow thawing produces little cell damage. Microwave defrosting is faster, but not as good; use only just before cooking. Meat can be cooked from frozen but generally yields inconsistent results.

Thawing times will vary depending on the shape and size of the cut. Once meat is defrosted it must not be left out at room temperature, since the quality deteriorates rapidly. Meat should not be re-frozen after it has thawed, except in emergencies. If ice crystals are still present in the meat, it can be refrozen. If meat is completely thawed it should be cooked before being refrozen.

FREEZING GAME

Game should be field dressed, then refrigerated until further processing and freezing. The meat can be aged for in the refrigerator for 1 to 3 weeks, wrapped in a wet shroud to prevent dehydration.

Small game like rabbits need to be skinned, dressed, cooled and cut into serving portions before freezing.

How to freeze poultry

Fresh poultry needs to be washed and dried, with giblets and neck removed before freezing. Freezing stuffed poultry in a home freezer is not recommended; freeze stuffing separately.

PACKAGING

To prevent freezer burn, wrap poultry in moisture-proof freezer wrap. Chicken pieces and whole birds can also be conveniently frozen in freezer bags. Try to remove as much air as possible before sealing.

Chicken purchased already wrapped and on trays can be frozen in that wrap for up to 2 weeks. For longer storage, it should be re-wrapped in moisture/vapor-resistant wrap or placed in a freezer bag.

THAWING

Poultry is best thawed in the refrigerator. Allow approximately 5 hours defrosting time in the fridge for each 1 lb (500 g). If you're pressed for time, thaw poultry in cold water in the sink; add more cold water periodically to keep temperature cold. Once thawed, poultry should not be refrozen.

FREEZING GAME BIRDS

Freshly killed game birds should be bled and cooled as quickly as possible, then plucked, eviscerated, cut into serving pieces, packaged and frozen immediately. (Be sure to remove any shot pellets before freezing!) Thaw as you would for poultry.

How to freeze fish

Freezing is a convenient way to preserve fresh fish – and is invaluable for the avid fisherman.

In general, fish cannot be frozen for as long as meat because it contains polyunsaturated fats that are uniformly distributed throughout the flesh. These fats are easily oxidized, which leads to a rancid odor and brownish color.

The higher the fat level, the shorter the freezer life. High-fat fish can only be frozen for 2 months. Medium and lean fish can be frozen for up to 3 or 4 months.

Lean fish include haddock, ocean perch, freshwater perch, pickerel, pike, smelt and shellfish.

Medium-fat fish include halibut, whitefish, speckled trout, rainbow trout.

High-fat fish include salmon, lake trout, mackerel, shad, turbot, tuna, Alaska black cod, and barbotte.

PREPARING FISH FOR FREEZING

Whole fish must be scaled before freezing. First wipe fish with a damp cloth. Hold the tail of the fish and, with a dull knife at a 45-degree angle, scale the fish from tail to head under running tap water.

To extend storage life, lean fish can be soaked in a brine solution of 1 cup (250 mL) coarse salt to 1 gallon (4 L) water for 20 seconds. Fat fish should be dipped in a solution of 1 1/2 tbsp (20 mL) ascorbic acid mixed in 1 quart (1 L) cold water.

PACKAGING AND FREEZING FISH

Depending on the type, fish can be frozen whole, filleted or cut into steaks.

For **lake trout, salmon** and **whitefish**, freeze whole. To help retain quality, "glaze" the fish with ice: Dip fish as soon as it is frozen into ice cold water, then return to the freezer; repeat this process several times until there is a glaze of ice over the fish.

Wrap frozen whole fish in freezer paper or in freezer bags; date and label. For fish steaks, cut from the center of the fish into thicknesses of 1/2 inch (1 cm) to 1 inch (2 cm). Wrap, date and label.

Fish should be frozen quickly at -10° F (-23° C) or colder. If your freezer cannot maintain this temperature, ask your fishmonger to freeze the fish for you before you take it home.

Once frozen, it is essential that fish be kept frozen at a constant temperature to maintain quality.

Slow freezing, fluctuating freezing temperatures and poor wrapping result in freezer burn, toughness, off flavors and lack of juiciness.

COOKING FISH

Because it contains only a small amount of connective tissue, fish can be cooked from frozen quickly, at high heat, for delicious, juicy results. Preheat oven to 450° F (230° C). Measure fish at the thickest part. For each 1 inch (2.5 cm) thickness, bake 20 minutes from frozen or 10 minutes from thawed. (For other cooking methods, such as frying or poaching, fish must be thawed.)

Fish is cooked when the flesh appears opaque or milky and it flakes easily with a fork. Fish cools quickly, so it is best served immediately on heated plates.

harvest freezer

Antipasto

4	carrots, diced	4
2	red bell peppers, diced	2
2	zucchini, diced	2
1	cauliflower, finely chopped	1
1	large onion, chopped	1
2	cloves garlic, minced	2
2 cups	ketchup	500 mL
2/3 cup	horseradish	175 mL
1/2 cup	vegetable oil	125 mL
1/2 cup	cider vinegar	125 mL
1	jar (12 oz [375 mL]) pimento-stuffed olives, drained and coarsely chopped	1
1	can (12 oz [375 mL]) black olives, dried and coarsely chopped (optional)	1
1	jar (6 oz [170 mL]) marinated artichokes, liquid drained and reserved, coarsely chopped	1
1	bay leaf	1
1/2 cup	chopped fresh parsley	125 mL
2 tsp	dried basil (or 2 tbsp [25 mL] fresh or frozen basil)	10 mL
1/4 tsp	hot pepper sauce (or more to taste)	1 mL

AFTER FREEZING/BEFORE SERVING

2	cans (6.5 oz [170 g]) water-packed flaked tuna, drained (added at time of serving)	2

1. In steamer basket set over large pot of boiling water, individually steam carrots, peppers, zucchini and cauliflower until tender-crisp.

2. In large stainless steel saucepan, combine onions, garlic, ketchup, oil, vinegar, olives (if using), artichokes, parsley, horseradish, basil and hot pepper sauce. Bring to a boil; reduce heat and simmer for 5 minutes. Stir in steamed vegetables; simmer for another 15 minutes. Remove from heat and allow to cool completely. Discard bay leaf.

To freeze: Pack into preserving jars or containers of usable size, leaving required headspace (see page 25); seal, date and label. Freeze for up to 6 months.

To serve: Thaw in refrigerator overnight. Stir in drained tuna. Serve with crackers.

Sweet Onion and Tomato Soup with Fresh Basil Crème

SERVES 6

The perfect choice when you're pressed for time, this soup tastes like it's made with freshly picked tomatoes. No one need ever know they've come from a can!

FREEZER TIP

You can use tomatoes from the freezer for the base of this soup.

From Marilyn Crowley and Joan Mackie: The Best Soup Cookbook

2 tbsp	butter	25 mL
1	large Spanish onion, diced	1
4 cups	chicken stock	1 L
1	can (28 oz [796 mL]) diced tomatoes, including juice	1
1/4 tsp	cayenne	1 mL
AFTER FREEZING/BEFORE SERVING		
1/2 cup	whipping (35%) cream, softly whipped	125 mL
2 tbsp	finely chopped fresh basil	25 mL
	Crunchy Wedges (see recipe, page 43)	

1. In a large saucepan, heat butter over medium heat. Add onion and cook for 15 minutes or until lightly browned. Add stock, tomatoes (with juice) and cayenne; bring to a boil. Reduce heat and simmer, covered and stirring occasionally, for 20 minutes.

2. In a blender or food processor, purée soup in batches. *If freezing soup, see "to freeze" section below; otherwise proceed with Step 3.*

3. Return to saucepan and heat until hot. In a bowl stir together whipped cream and basil. Ladle soup into warmed soup bowls; garnish with a dollop of basil crème. Pass a basket of Crunchy Wedges.

To freeze: Cool. Ladle into freezer containers. Seal, label and date. Freeze for up to 4 months.

To serve: Thaw soup in microwave or in refrigerator overnight. Proceed with Step 3, above.

Crunchy Wedges

PREHEAT OVEN TO 350° F (180° C)
BAKING SHEET

2 tbsp	melted butter *or* olive oil (or a combination of both)	25 mL
4	small (6-inch [15 cm]) pita breads	4

MAKES 64 SMALL WEDGES

Pita breads, as a visit to most supermarkets proves, have gone from exotic to mainstream in recent years. They are an extremely versatile staple, and may be turned into a variety of delicious nibblers to accompany soups. Choose a recipe that will complement the flavors in the soup.

Make a large batch and freeze in tightly sealed freezer bags, all well-labeled with the flavor and date for future reference.

VARIATIONS

Salt Lover's: Pinches of coarse or sea salt

Zippy: 2 tbsp (25 mL) finely chopped fresh coriander and pinches of cayenne

Herbed: 1 1/2 tsp (7 mL) mixed dried herbs such as basil, oregano and rosemary.

From Marilyn Crowley and Joan Mackie: *The Best Soup Cookbook*

1. Lightly brush melted butter over both sides of pita; cut into 8 wedges. Split pieces, forming 2 thinner wedges. Place rough-side down in a single layer on baking sheet. If desired, sprinkle with the ingredients for one of the variations given below. Bake, stirring once, for 10 to 15 minutes or until golden brown and crisp. Set aside to cool before using. If stored wedges lose crispness, spread out on a baking sheet; bake at 300° F (150° C) for 3 to 5 minutes or just until hot and crisp.

Pea and Asparagus Soup with Fresh Tarragon

From Marilyn Crowley and
Joan Mackie: *The Best Soup
Cookbook*

SERVES 6 TO 8

This easy-to-make soup is lively with fresh vegetables and has a velvety smooth texture. Better yet, it's almost fat-free! A bowl of this soup is the closest thing you'll find to eating freshly shelled peas just plucked from the vine.

The slightly smoky flavor of this soup comes from tarragon – a perennial herb that grows as tall as 3 feet (90 cm) and is known to the French as the King of Herbs. Its mysterious anise flavor is often paired with poultry, veal and eggs.

FREEZER TIP

Frozen peas and asparagus work well in this soup.

Fresh tarragon is not always available throughout the year. But you can always have some on hand in the freezer. Just chop fresh tarragon, wrap it in plastic wrap, and store in a freezer container for up to 1 year.

2 lbs	asparagus, trimmed and cut into 2-inch (5 cm) pieces	1 kg
2 cups	fresh or frozen peas	500 mL
6 cups	vegetable stock or chicken stock	1.5 L
1 tbsp	chopped fresh tarragon	15 mL
1/2 tsp	salt	2 mL
1/4 tsp	black pepper	1 mL
AFTER FREEZING/BEFORE SERVING		
1 cup	Rye Croutons (see recipe, page 45)	250 mL

1. In a large saucepan over high heat, combine asparagus, peas, stock, tarragon, salt and pepper; bring to a boil. Reduce heat and simmer for 10 minutes or until asparagus is very tender.

2. In a blender or food processor, purée soup in batches. *If freezing soup, see "to freeze" section below; otherwise proceed with Step 3.*

3. Return to saucepan and heat until hot. Ladle into warmed soup bowls; garnish with Rye Croutons.

To freeze: Cool. Ladle into freezer containers. Seal, label and date. Freeze for up to 4 months.

To serve: Thaw soup in microwave or in refrigerator overnight. Proceed with Step 3, above.

Rye Croutons

MAKES ABOUT 2 1/2 CUPS (625 mL)

Croutons were first created by thrifty cooks looking for ways to use up bread trimmings. Here we have a basic crouton recipe, with variations to provide you with an assortment of flavors to try as lively toppings for all sorts of soups.

Use leftover rye bread or just about any other kind of bread, including French (baguette), pumpernickel or whole wheat. Remember that day-old bread slices more easily than fresh.

From Marilyn Crowley and Joan Mackie: *The Best Soup Cookbook*

FREEZER TIP

The croutons keep well, stored in tightly sealed bags in the freezer. Be sure to label them so you know what flavors you have put away.

PREHEAT OVEN TO 350° F (180° C)
BAKING SHEET

1/4 cup	melted butter or olive oil (or a combination of both)	50 mL
8	slices rye bread, crusts removed and cubed	8
	(about 2 1/2 cups [625 mL])	

1. In a bowl stir together butter or oil and, if desired, the ingredients for one of the variations below. Add bread cubes; toss until lightly coated. Spread in a single layer on baking sheet (or shallow baking dish). Bake, stirring once, for 10 to 15 minutes or until golden brown and crisp. Set aside to cool before using. If stored croutons lose crispness, spread out on a baking sheet; bake at 300° F (150° C) for 3 to 5 minutes or just until hot and crisp.

Yellow Pepper Soup with Fresh Tomato Salsa

PREHEAT BROILER OR BARBECUE GRILL

SERVES 4

All too often we see diced peppers garnishing tomato soup, so here's something of a role-reversal – a bell pepper soup complimented with a topping of spicy, crunchy tomato salsa. In keeping with the golden color of the saffron used to spice the soup, we decided to use yellow peppers here – but red or orange peppers can be used just as successfully.

FREEZER TIP

Freeze yellow peppers and tomatoes when they are abundant and inexpensive in the fall. They work perfectly in this recipe.

From Marilyn Crowley and Joan Mackie, *The Best Soup Cookbook*

4	large yellow bell peppers	4
1 tbsp	butter	15 mL
1	onion, diced	1
1	large clove garlic, minced	1
2 cups	chicken stock	500 mL
1	large carrot, sliced	1
1	small banana or jalapeño pepper, seeded	1
1/4 tsp	saffron threads, crumbled	1 mL
AFTER FREEZING/BEFORE SERVING		
1 cup	half-and-half (10%) cream	250 mL
1/2 cup	Fresh Salsa Topping (see recipe, page 47)	125 mL

1. Under broiler or on barbecue grill, roast peppers, turning occasionally, for 15 minutes or until skins are charred black. Place in a paper bag; close and leave in bag for 10 minutes. Peel and cut in half. Reserving juice, discard the stem, skin and seeds.

2. In a large saucepan, melt butter over medium heat. Add onion and garlic; cook for 5 minutes or until onion has softened. Stir in stock, carrot, roasted peppers (including juices) and banana pepper. Crumble in saffron; bring to a boil. Reduce heat and simmer, covered, for 20 minutes or until vegetables are very tender.

3. In a blender or food processor, purée soup in batches. *If freezing soup, see "To freeze" section below; otherwise proceed with Step 4.*

4. Transfer soup to a bowl and chill, covered, for 6 hours or overnight. When ready to serve, stir in cream. Taste and adjust seasoning as needed. Ladle into chilled soup bowls; serve garnished with a spoonful of Fresh Salsa.

To freeze: Cool. Ladle into freezer containers. Seal, label and date. Freeze for up to 4 months.

To serve: Thaw soup in microwave or in refrigerator overnight. Proceed with Step 4, above.

Fresh Salsa Topping

MAKES 1 CUP (250 mL)

For a perky pepper-upper to soups, fish and meats, salsas can't be topped. They should be a bit hot and tangy and they are best served soon after making. (Have you never tasted a fresh salsa? The difference between this and the bottled variety is startling.)

Try adding a small spoonful of olive oil to the salsa and you'll make a terrific dip for tortilla chips.

From Marilyn Crowley and Joan Mackie: *The Best Soup Cookbook*

3 or 4	plum tomatoes, seeded and finely diced	3 or 4
1/4 cup	finely minced sweet or red onion	50 mL
1	clove garlic, minced	1
1	small hot pepper (such as poblano or jalapeño) seeded and finely minced or 1/4 tsp (1 mL) hot pepper sauce	1
1 tbsp	chopped fresh coriander	15 mL
1 to 2 tsp	lime juice	5 to 10 mL
1/8 tsp	salt	0.5 mL

1. In a bowl stir together tomatoes, onion, garlic, hot pepper, coriander, half of the lime juice and salt. Let stand at room temperature for 30 minutes. Taste and, if desired, add remaining lime juice. Use at once or refrigerate, covered, for up to 1 day. Add a spoonful to garnish freshly made soup or to perk up the flavor of defrosted soups.

Beef-Stuffed Spuds

SERVES 4

Baked potatoes stuffed with a variety of fillings is a popular meal in my house. I make them ahead for those nights when everyone is on a different schedule. The potatoes need only a quick reheat in the microwave as each person walks through the door for an instant supper.

TIP

How to bake potatoes. Scrub baking potatoes (10 oz [300 g] each) well and pierce skins with a fork in several places to allow steam to escape. To oven bake: Place in 400° F (200° C) oven for 1 hour or until potatoes give slightly when squeezed. To microwave: Arrange potatoes in a circle, spacing 1-inch (2.5 cm) apart on roasting rack or on a paper towel in microwave oven. Microwave at High, turning over halfway through cooking, until potatoes are just tender when pierced with a skewer.

4	large baking potatoes (about 10 oz [300 g] each)	4
8 oz	lean ground beef or ground veal	250 g
1/3 cup	finely chopped onions	75 mL
1	clove garlic, minced	1
1 tsp	Worcestershire sauce	5 mL
	Salt and pepper	
1/2 cup	sour cream or plain yogurt or buttermilk (approximate)	125 mL
1 cup	shredded Cheddar cheese	250 mL
2 tbsp	chopped parsley	25 mL

1. Bake or microwave potatoes as directed (see Tip, at left).

2. In a large nonstick skillet over medium-high heat, cook beef, breaking up with back of spoon, for 4 minutes or until no longer pink.

3. Reduce heat to medium. Add onions, garlic and Worcestershire sauce; season with salt and pepper. Cook, stirring often, for 4 minutes or until onions are softened.

4. Cut warm potatoes in half lengthwise. Carefully scoop out each potato, leaving a 1/4-inch (5 mm) shell; set shells aside.

5. In a bowl mash potatoes with potato masher or fork; beat in enough sour cream until smooth. Stir in beef mixture, half the cheese and all the parsley; season with salt and pepper to taste. Spoon into potato shells; top with remaining cheese.

Microwave cooking times at High: 1 potato, 4 to 5 minutes; 2 potatoes, 6 to 8 minutes; 4 potatoes, 10 to 12 minutes

For moist potatoes wrap cooked potatoes individually in foil. For drier potatoes, wrap in a dry towel. Let stand 5 minutes.

From Johanna Burkhard: *The Comfort Food Cookbook*

6. Arrange in shallow baking dish; bake in preheated oven for 15 minutes or until cheese is melted. Or place on microwave-safe rack or large serving plate; microwave at Medium-High for 5 to 7 minutes or until heated through and cheese melts.

To freeze: Cool. Wrap individually in plastic wrap, then in foil. freeze for up to 2 months.

To serve: Thaw in refrigerator overnight. Unwrap and bake in a preheated 350° F (180° C) oven for about 20 minutes or until heated through.

Broccoli and Cheese-Stuffed Potatoes

PREHEAT OVEN TO 400° F (200° C)
SHALLOW BAKING DISH

SERVES 4

These delicious baked potatoes are great to pack along to work if you have the use of a microwave for reheating.

TIP

Cheddar and broccoli are a classic combo, but get adventurous with whatever cheese and vegetables are in the fridge. Another favorite is mozzarella cheese and lightly sautéed mushrooms and diced red peppers seasoned with basil.

From Johanna Burkhard: *The Comfort Food Cookbook*

4	large baking potatoes (about 10 oz [300 g] each)	4
3 cups	small broccoli florets and peeled, chopped stems	750 mL
1/2 cup	sour cream or plain yogurt or buttermilk (approximate)	125 mL
2	green onions, chopped	2
1 1/3 cups	shredded Cheddar or Gruyere cheese	325 mL
	Salt and cayenne pepper	

1. Bake or microwave potatoes as directed (see Tip, pages 48 to 49).

2. In a saucepan cook or steam broccoli until just crisp-tender. (Or place in covered casserole and microwave at High for 3 minutes.) Drain well.

3. Cut a thin slice from tops of warm potatoes. Scoop out potato leaving a 1/4-inch (5 mm) shell, being careful not to tear the skins.

4. In a bowl mash potato with potato masher or fork; beat in enough sour cream until smooth. Add broccoli, onion and 1 cup (250 mL) of the cheese. Season with salt and a dash of cayenne pepper to taste.

5. Spoon filling into potato shells, mounding the tops. Arrange in shallow baking dish; sprinkle with remaining cheese. Bake in preheated oven for 20 minutes or until cheese melts. Or place on a rack and microwave at Medium-High for 5 to 7 minutes or until heated through and cheese melts.

To freeze: Cool. Wrap individually in plastic wrap, then in foil. freeze for up to 2 months.

To serve: Thaw in refrigerator overnight. Unwrap and bake in a preheated 350° F (180° C) oven for about 20 minutes or until heated through.

Green Beans Stewed with Tomatoes

SERVES 4

This is a favorite dish to make in late summer when young beans and ripe tomatoes are at their best. But even in winter, with vine-ripened greenhouse tomatoes and imported fresh beans, this recipe is still good. If bits of tomato skin in the sauce bother you, peel the tomatoes before dicing.

TIP

For a quick supper, toss vegetable sauce with 8 oz (250 g) cooked pasta (such as penne) and sprinkle generously with Parmesan cheese. Also substitute other vegetables – such as fennel, asparagus or broccoli – for the beans.

From Johanna Burkhard: *The Comfort Food Cookbook*

1 lb	green beans	500 g
1 tbsp	olive oil	15 mL
1	small red onion, halved lengthwise, thinly sliced	1
2	cloves garlic, thinly sliced	2
1 tsp	dried basil	5 mL
2	ripe tomatoes, diced	2
1 tbsp	balsamic vinegar	15 mL
2 tbsp	water (approximate)	25 mL
1/4 tsp	salt	1 mL
1/4 tsp	pepper	1 mL
	Water	

1. Trim ends of beans; cut into 1 1/2-inch (4 cm) lengths. In a saucepan, cook beans in lightly salted boiling water, for 3 to 4 minutes (start timing when water returns to a boil) or until still crisp. Drain well; reserve.

2. Meanwhile, in a large nonstick skillet, heat oil over medium heat. Add onion, garlic and basil; cook, stirring, for 2 minutes or until softened.

3. Stir in tomatoes, vinegar, 2 tbsp (25 mL) water, salt and pepper; cook, stirring often, for 3 minutes or until sauce-like.

4. Add beans; cover and simmer for 8 to 10 minutes, stirring occasionally, until tender. Add more water, if necessary, to keep mixture moist. Serve warm or at room temperature.

To freeze: Cool. Spoon into freezer container; seal, date and label. Freeze for up to 4 months.

To serve: Thaw in refrigerator overnight. Reheat or serve at room temperature.

Sweet-and-Sour Red Cabbage with Apples

SERVES 8

I consider this recipe a convenience food. I keep containers of sweet-and-sour red cabbage in my freezer, ready to microwave at a moment's notice to serve along with pork chops or roasts.

TIP

Depending on how sweet-and-sour you like your red cabbage, add more brown sugar and vinegar to taste. Most cooked red cabbage recipes, this one included, call for vinegar or wine. This adds not only flavor, but acidity, which preserves the cabbage's bright red color.

From Johanna Burkhard: *The Comfort Food Cookbook*

2 tbsp	butter	25 mL
1	large onion, finely chopped	1
2	apples, peeled, cored and diced	2
1 cup	chicken stock *or* vegetable stock	250 mL
1/2 cup	red wine *or* additional stock	125 mL
1/3 cup	red wine vinegar	75 mL
1/3 cup	packed brown sugar	75 mL
1	bay leaf	1
1/2 tsp	salt	2 mL
1/4 tsp	cinnamon	1 mL
1/4 tsp	pepper	1 mL
Pinch	ground cloves	Pinch
1	medium red cabbage, finely shredded (about 10 cups [2.5 L])	1
1 1/2 tsp	cornstarch	7 mL
1 tbsp	cold water	15 mL

1. In a Dutch oven, heat butter over medium heat. Add onions and apples; cook, stirring often, for 5 minutes or until softened.

2. Add stock, wine, vinegar, brown sugar, bay leaf, salt, cinnamon, pepper and ground cloves. Bring to a boil; stir in cabbage.

3. Cover and simmer over medium-low heat, stirring occasionally, for 45 minutes or until cabbage is tender.

4. Blend cornstarch with water; stir into cabbage. Cook 3 minutes more or until sauce is slightly thickened. Remove bay leaf before serving.

To freeze: Cool. Spoon into freezer container; seal, date and label. Freeze for up to 3 months.

To serve: Thaw in refrigerator overnight. Reheat.

Veggie, Beef and Pasta Bake

PREHEAT OVEN TO 350° F (180° C)
13- BY 9-INCH (3 L) BAKING DISH, GREASED

SERVES 6

Here's a terrific recipe that makes a complete meal, with something from all 4 food groups! The pasta does not require any pre-cooking so you save preparation and clean-up time.

TIP

If you are concerned about sodium, use light soya sauce instead of the regular variety. One tbsp (15 mL) regular soya sauce contains 1037 mg sodium; the same amount of sodium-reduced or light soya sauce contains only 605 mg.

FREEZER TIP

This quick family meal is even faster to make when you have tomatoes and zucchini handy in the freezer. Vegetables will freeze well for up to 1 year.

From Dietitians of Canada: Great Food Fast

1 lb	lean ground beef	500 g
1 cup	sliced onions	250 mL
1 cup	diced zucchini	250 mL
2 tsp	minced garlic	10 mL
1	can (28 oz [796 mL]) stewed or diced tomatoes, with juice	1
2 tbsp	sodium-reduced soya sauce	25 mL
1/2 tsp	crushed red pepper flakes	2 mL
2 cups	rotini (or other spiral pasta)	500 mL
1 1/2 cups	shredded Cheddar cheese	375 mL

1. In a large nonstick skillet over medium-high heat, combine ground beef, onions, zucchini and garlic; cook for 8 to 10 minutes or until beef is no longer pink and vegetables are softened. Drain fat; pour beef mixture into baking dish. Set aside.

2. Meanwhile, drain juice from tomatoes into an 8-cup (2 L) microwave-safe measuring cup; add water to make 2 cups (500 mL). Roughly chop tomatoes; add to measuring cup. Stir in soya sauce and red pepper flakes. Microwave on High for 5 minutes or until very hot. Stir in rotini.

3. Pour tomato-pasta mixture into baking dish and combine with meat mixture. Press pasta down to make sure it is submerged in the liquid. Bake in preheated oven, covered, for 20 minutes. Remove cover; stir gently and sprinkle with cheese. Bake, uncovered, for 15 to 20 minutes or until pasta is tender.

To freeze: Wrap well in plastic wrap, then foil. Freeze for up to 3 months.

To serve: Thaw in microwave or in refrigerator overnight. Preheat oven to 350° F (180° C). Unwrap and bake, uncovered, for 40 to 45 minutes or until bubbly.

Basil Pesto

**MAKES ABOUT
1 1/3 CUPS
(325 mL)**

Keep a jar of this classic Italian sauce in your freezer. Use on pasta, with added vinegar as a salad dressing, as a sauce for fish or chicken, or on croustades (see page 128).

TIP

Store in freezer in a well sealed plastic container away from delicately flavored foods to avoid transferring the garlic flavor and smell to other foods.

If you don't think you will use a whole batch at a time, divide and freeze in separate containers of, say, 1/3 cup (75 mL) each.

1/4 cup	pine nuts	50 mL
2 cups	packed fresh basil leaves	500 mL
1/2 cup	grated Parmesan cheese	125 mL
3	cloves garlic, chopped	3
1/2 tsp	salt	2 mL
1/4 tsp	freshly ground black pepper	1 mL
3/4 cup	extra virgin olive oil	175 mL

1. Spread pine nuts on baking sheet. Toast for 10 minutes or until golden and fragrant. Cool.

2. In food processor, combine pine nuts, basil, cheese, garlic, salt and pepper. Process until finely chopped.

3. With motor running, add oil through the feed tube until pesto is emulsified.

To freeze: Spoon into small jars and freeze for up to 2 months.

To serve: Thaw in refrigerator overnight or in microwave.

Thyme Butter

MAKES 1/2 CUP (125 mL)

Give your grilled steak, fish, chicken or vegetable sizzle with a pat of herb butter, "fresh" from the freezer. Instead of garlic bread, why not try a garlic herb butter in a crusty loaf?

VARIATIONS

Use chopped dill, tarragon, sage or basil instead of thyme.

Pesto Sun-Dried Tomato Butter: Omit thyme. Add 3 tbsp (45 mL) chopped basil and 2 tbsp (25 mL) chopped oil-packed sun-dried tomatoes. Use over hot pasta.

1/2 cup	butter, softened	125 mL
1/4 cup	chopped fresh thyme	50 mL
1	small clove garlic, minced	1

1. In a small bowl with an electric mixer, beat together butter, thyme and garlic until well combined. Spoon onto piece of plastic wrap. Roll up to encase in a 1 1/2-inch (4 cm) diameter log.

To freeze: Place log in freezer bag; seal, date and label. Freeze for up to 1 month.

To use: Unwrap log and cut off 1/4-inch (5 mm) slices. Use to flavor hot foods or bread.

Tarragon Herb Butter

**MAKES ABOUT
3/4 CUP
(175 mL)**

This flavorful butter has many uses, but is particularly good with boneless skinless chicken breasts (see below).

Chicken Breasts Stuffed with Tarragon Herb Butter. Preheat oven to 350° F (180° C). Cut Tarragon Herb Butter log into slices and distribute slices between 6 to 8 single boneless skinless chicken breasts, laying the slices at the center of each breast. Fold chicken around butter; dredge chicken breasts in breadcrumbs and arrange in baking dish. Bake uncovered for 40 to 45 minutes or until juices run clear when chicken is pierced with a fork. Serve immediately.

1/2 cup	butter, softened	125 mL
1/2 cup	chopped fresh parsley	125 mL
2 tbsp	chopped fresh tarragon	25 mL
1	clove garlic, crushed	1

1. In small bowl, beat together butter, parsley, tarragon and garlic until well combined. Shape into a log with a 1/2-inch (1 cm) diameter. Wrap log in plastic.

To freeze: Place log in freezer bag; seal, date and label. Freeze for up to 1 month.

To use: Unwrap log and cut off 1/4-inch (5 mm) slices. Use to flavor hot foods or bread.

Cranberry-Orange Chutney

MAKES ABOUT 4 CUPS (1 L)

This festive chutney is the perfect accompaniment to the rich flavors of tourtiere, a Christmas turkey or ham. Extra jars make wonderful hostess gifts.

1	bag (3 cups [750 mL]) fresh or frozen cranberries	1
2	onions, chopped	2
1 cup	raisins or currants	250 mL
3/4 cup	granulated sugar	175 mL
3/4 cup	packed brown sugar	175 mL
	Finely grated zest and juice from 1 orange	
1 cup	cider vinegar	250 mL
1 tsp	ground cinnamon	5 mL
1 tsp	ground cloves	5 mL
1 tsp	ground ginger	5 mL
1 tsp	salt	5 mL

1. In a large stainless steel saucepan, combine cranberries, onions, raisins, granulated sugar, brown sugar, orange zest and juice, vinegar, cinnamon, cloves, ginger and salt. Bring to a boil. Reduce heat to simmer. Cook uncovered, stirring frequently, for 20 to 25 minutes or until thickened.

To freeze: Allow to cool completely. Spoon into containers and freeze for up to 1 year.

To serve: Thaw in refrigerator overnight.

Rhubarb Chutney

MAKES ABOUT 8 CUPS (2 L)

A batch of this recipe has many uses. It is delicious served with cream cheese and crackers, as a glaze for barbecued pork or poultry and as a condiment with any pork or poultry dish. Feel free to halve the recipe to makes it more manageable.

10 cups	coarsely chopped rhubarb, fresh or frozen	2.5 L
2 cups	chopped onions	500 mL
2 cups	cider vinegar	500 mL
1 1/2 cups	granulated sugar	375 mL
1 1/2 cups	packed brown sugar	375 mL
1 cup	raisins	250 mL
1 cup	currants	250 mL
1/2 cup	chopped crystallized ginger	125 mL
1 tsp	salt	5 mL
1 tsp	ground cinnamon	5 mL
1 tsp	ground cloves	5 mL
1 tsp	curry powder	5 mL

1. In a large stainless steel saucepan, combine rhubarb, onions, vinegar, sugars, raisins, currants, ginger, salt, cinnamon, cloves and curry powder. Bring to a boil. Reduce heat to simmer; cook uncovered for 20 to 25 minutes, stirring frequently, or until thickened.

2. Remove from heat and allow to cool to room temperature.

To freeze: Allow to cool completely. Spoon into containers and freeze for up to 1 year.

To serve: Thaw in refrigerator overnight.

Strawberry Preserves

**MAKES ABOUT
4 CUPS (1 L)**

This is a cheater's preserve – actually more like a sauce than a true preserve. Still, it tastes wonderful and no one needs to know it was simply made from frozen berries!

TIP

When packing berries for the freezer, remember to mark the quantity of fresh berries on the freezer bag, since they expand on freezing.

VARIATION

Substitute blueberries or raspberries for strawberries in this recipe.

4 cups	frozen unsweetened strawberries	1 L
3/4 cup	granulated sugar	175 mL
1 tbsp	cornstarch	15 mL

1. In a large saucepan, stir together strawberries, sugar and cornstarch. Cook over medium-high heat for 3 to 5 minutes, stirring constantly, or until thickened and clear.

2. Remove from heat and allow to cool to room temperature.

To freeze: Transfer cooled preserves to rigid plastic containers or preserving jars leaving required headspace (see page 25). Freeze for up to 6 months.

To serve: Thaw in refrigerator overnight.

Raspberry Sauce

**MAKES ABOUT
2 CUPS (500 mL)**

A versatile dessert sauce
which is excellent over ice
cream or cake.

TIP

If using frozen raspberries,
be sure to buy the individually frozen type, not the
ones packed in syrup.
When freezing berries,
mark the unfrozen quantity
on the freezer bag as they
expand on freezing.

2 cups	fresh or frozen raspberries	500 mL
1/4 cup	granulated sugar	50 mL
1 tbsp	cornstarch (optional)	15 mL

1. In a saucepan combine raspberries, sugar and, if
   using, cornstarch. Cook over low heat until clear and
   thickened.

2. Force warm sauce through a fine-mesh sieve to remove
   seeds. Cool.

To freeze: Transfer cooled sauce to freezer container. Freeze for
up to 6 months.

To serve: Thaw in refrigerator overnight.

Freezer Fruit Pie

MAKES 1 PIE

Everyone loves an old-fashioned fruit pie. This one is a cinch to make using 2 frozen pie shells and a homemade frozen fruit filling.

VARIATION

Try making the fruit filling with peaches or berries. If using berries, replace brown sugar with granulated sugar.

9-INCH (23 CM) FOIL PIE PLATE

FRUIT FILLING

6 cups	sliced peeled apples	1 1/2 L
3/4 cup	packed brown sugar	175 mL
4 tbsp	all-purpose flour	50 mL
1 tsp	ground cinnamon	5 mL
1/2 tsp	ground nutmeg	2 mL

AFTER FREEZING/BEFORE SERVING

2	9-inch (23 cm) pie shells	2

1. In a bowl stir together apples, brown sugar, flour, cinnamon and nutmeg until well combined. Spoon filling into foil pie plate.

To freeze: Wrap pie plate with heavy foil. Date, label and freeze for up to 6 months.

To serve: Preheat oven to 425° F (220° C). Pop filling out and place in one of the pie shells. Place second pie shell on top and crimp edges together. Transfer to baking sheet and bake for 15 minutes. Reduce heat to 375° F (190° C) and bake another 35 to 45 minutes or until filling is bubbling.

Rhubarb-Strawberry Cobbler with Candied Ginger

PREHEAT OVEN TO 375° F (190° C)
8-INCH (2 L) SQUARE BAKING DISH

SERVES 6

You can omit the ginger from this old-fashioned dessert if you prefer, but it goes beautifully with the rhubarb and adds a flavor boost to the crème fraîche.

KITCHEN WISDOM

In its native France, crème fraîche was traditionally made by letting unpasteurized cream stand until it developed a slightly sour flavor. My method of making it is quicker – and safer – and the slightly tart flavor goes well with all kinds of desserts.

Look for candied ginger in the jams and jellies section of your supermarket or in your local bulk food store. Try it finely chopped over fresh cantaloupe or stirred into a fruit salad.

FRUIT LAYER

4 cups	sliced fresh rhubarb (about 1 lb [500 g]) or frozen rhubarb, partially thawed and patted dry	1 L
2 cups	hulled sliced strawberries	500 mL
1/4 cup	granulated sugar	50 mL
1/4 cup	finely chopped candied ginger in syrup, drained (reserve syrup for crème fraîche)	50 mL
1 tbsp	all-purpose flour	15 mL

TOPPING

1 cup	all-purpose flour	250 mL
3 tbsp	granulated sugar	45 mL
2 tsp	baking powder	10 mL
Pinch	salt	Pinch
1/4 cup	cold butter, cut into pieces	50 mL
3/4 cup	sour cream	175 mL

GINGER CRÈME FRAÎCHE

1/3 cup	whipping (35%) cream	75 mL
2/3 cup	sour cream	150 mL
2 tbsp	ginger syrup (reserved from candied ginger)	25 mL

1. Fruit Layer: In baking dish, stir together rhubarb, strawberries, sugar, ginger and flour. Set aside.

2. Topping: In a food processor, combine flour, 2 tbsp (25 mL) sugar, baking powder and salt; process until combined. Add butter; process until mixture resembles fine crumbs. Add sour cream; process until a soft sticky dough forms.

FREEZER TIP

Nothing tastes sweeter in mid-winter than the delectable flavor of "fresh" strawberries and rhubarb from your freezer. Fruit freezes well and keeps for up to 1 year.

From Julia Aitken: *Easy Entertaining*

3. Drop dough in 6 spoonfuls evenly over fruit in baking dish. (Fruit will not be completely covered.) Sprinkle evenly with remaining sugar. Bake in preheated oven for 35 to 40 minutes or until topping has risen and is golden brown, and fruit is bubbly. Serve warm with Ginger Crème Fraîche.

4. Ginger Crème Fraîche: Place a medium bowl and the beaters of electric mixer in the freezer; chill for 15 minutes. Pour whipping cream into chilled bowl; beat with electric mixer at high speed until soft peaks just start to form (cream should still be slightly runny). With a large spoon or rubber spatula and using a gentle, cutting motion, fold in sour cream and ginger syrup until well combined. Refrigerate until ready to serve.

To freeze: When cobbler has cooled, wrap baking dish with heavy foil. Transfer cooled sauce to freezer container. Date, label and freeze for up to 2 months.

To serve: Thaw cobbler and sauce in refrigerator overnight. In a saucepan, gently warm Ginger Crème Fraîche before serving

Banana-Berry Wake-Up Shake

SERVES 2
MAKES ABOUT
3 1/4 CUPS (800 mL)

Frozen sliced bananas work well in these shakes and help make them creamy. When bananas start to get brown, pop them in the freezer and take out as needed.

TIP

The vanilla yogurt used in these shake recipes (and in Sunny Orange Shake, see page 32) is higher in carbohydrate than most other yogurts. People with diabetes may want to choose a lower-carbohydrate brand.

MAKE AHEAD

Make these shakes the night before and you'll be ready for a quick morning meal to go.

NUTRITION FACTS

These shakes are packed with bone-building calcium. People who are allergic to milk or who are lactose intolerant can substitute a calcium-fortified soy beverage and soy yogurt.

From Dietitians of Canada:
Great Food Fast

1	banana	1
1 cup	fresh or frozen berries (any combination)	250 mL
1 cup	milk or vanilla-flavored soy beverage	250 mL
3/4 cup	lower-fat yogurt (vanilla or other flavor that complements berries)	175 mL

1. In a blender liquefy fruit with a small amount of the milk. Add remaining milk and yogurt; blend until smooth. If shake is too thick, add extra milk or soy beverage to achieve desired consistency.

FREEZER TIP

While you can't freeze the end result (in fact, it would take more time to thaw than prepare), this shake is an ideal way to use frozen bananas and berries. Simply thaw fruit in refrigerator the night before to soften slightly. Then peel banana and pop fruit into the blender.

RHUBARB STRAWBERRY COBBLER WITH CANDIED GINGER (PAGE 62) ➤
OVERLEAF: PEA AND ASPARAGUS SOUP WITH FRESH TARRAGON (PAGE 44)

weekday meals

≺ QUICK CHICKEN NOODLE SOUP (PAGE 74)

Meals at the ready

I t seems that life just keeps getting busier. So how do you find the time to provide your family with home-cooked meals throughout the week? It's actually easier than you might think. With your freezer and a little planning, you can have a variety of delicious meals, ready to heat, eat and enjoy.

In this chapter, you'll find recipes for soups, lunches and quick meals, as well as casseroles, pasta dishes, hearty stews, and sauces – all of which are well suited to freezing. But these are just the beginning. You can use the information in this book to determine which of your own favorite recipes will freeze well (see pages 11 to 16), and build an inventory of meals that will provide your family with a delicious variety of choices for weeks or months.

On pages 180 and 181, you'll find a Month of Meals chart that will give you an idea of how you can build your freezer inventory using the recipes in this book. Don't be intimidated by the prospect of preparing so many meals in advance. If you wish, start with just a few days' worth of meals, then work your way up to a larger inventory. You may surprise yourself. Once you start cooking a particular dish, you may find that you have enough to freeze for two separate meals – in which case, plan to have one on the first week and the other on the following week. Before long, you will have enough food prepared for two weeks.

When planning what to cook for the freezer, keep in mind the importance of variety. Nobody wants to eat stews or casseroles for nights in a row, no matter how good they are. You should also cook different foods for different seasons. In the summer, as they say, " the living is easy." Because fresh fruit and vegetables are readily available a fresh salad with a grilled main course with bread is simple, delicious and sufficient. It requires little freezer preparation apart from putting the planned food for the grill into the freezer. In the winter, meals require more preparation. Soups, stews and casseroles require cooking time.

Breakfasts and lunches can also be made ahead and frozen. Try a selection of breads, muffins and bagels. Freezing sandwiches is a big time-saver. Sandwiches can be frozen for up to 6 weeks. If packed frozen in a lunch bag in the morning, they will be thawed by noon. Frozen sandwiches need to buttered to maintain moistness. Sandwich fillings such as cream cheese, meat, cheese, peanut butter, salmon and tuna – all freeze well. Avoid egg salad sandwiches or crisp vegetables, which do not freeze well. Having sandwiches ready in the freezer ensures you will take an appealing, nutritious lunch to work or to school.

Turning one meal into two (or three)

Smart meal planning depends on making the most of your time. For example, let's say that you plan to cook a roast on Sunday. Buy a big one. Don't be shy. Make the most of specials on roasts and turkeys. A big roast dinner can produce several dinners in the same time it takes to produce one. Enjoy that evening and have "planned overs" (it sounds so much better than "leftovers") the next evening with a salad. Slice the remaining roast, then package, label and freeze it for a quick dinner to enjoy in the following week or month.

When preparing weekday meals for the freezer, here are some additional points to keep in mind:

- Freeze foods in amounts to be served at one time

- Freeze in freezer containers not waxed containers which melt (see tips on packaging, page 12)

- Note foods that do not freeze well (see page 11)

- Rice and pasta dishes should be undercooked slightly, since these dishes will be cooked again when heated. Be cautious about undercooking dishes that contain meat, however.

- High-fat dishes will go rancid quickly; freeze for short periods up to 1 month.

- Dishes with cream sauces may curdle during re-heating, stirring will be necessary to "smooth out" the sauce.

- Some foods, like meatloaf, can be frozen raw or cooked.

- Sandwiches with butter, cream cheese, cheese, peanut butter and meat fillings freeze well. Fillings with fresh vegetables, jelly and mayonnaise do not freeze well. Sandwiches can be well wrapped individually in freezer bags and frozen for up to 6 weeks.

Playing it safe

It is critical when freezing cooked dishes (as it is with raw foods) to maintain sanitary conditions at safe temperatures. The rule is: keep hot food hot and cold food cold. The dangerous temperatures between 40° F (4° C) and 140° F (60° C) are the temperatures that bacteria grow quickly. So be sure to cool food rapidly after preparation in the refrigerator, and freeze immediately.

Do not freeze food that has not been kept at the correct temperature. If in doubt, throw it out!

Rich Beef Stock

From Bill Jones and Stephen Wong: *New World Noodles*

PREHEAT OVEN TO 400° F (200° C)
LARGE ROASTING PAN

MAKES ABOUT 18 CUPS (4.5 L)

Slowly roasting the beef bones caramelizes their sugars and enriches this stock. Try not to burn the bones, or the stock will be bitter.

The stock will keep refrigerated for about 1 week or it can be frozen and kept for up to 2 months.

5 lb	beef bones (shin or neck), rinsed to remove any blood	2 kg
3	large onions, peeled and roughly chopped	3
3	carrots, peeled and roughly chopped	3
3	celery stalks, roughly chopped	3
1	head garlic	1
1/2 cup	tomato paste	125 mL
3	bay leaves	3
1	small handful thyme	1
1	small handful rosemary	1
1	small handful marjoram	1
1	bunch parsley stalks	1
5	whole black peppercorns	5
20 cups	water	5 L

1. Place bones in pan and roast until lightly golden, about 2 hours. Add vegetables and garlic and roast 1 hour. Add tomato paste, stirring to coat. Roast 30 minutes.

2. Place roasted bones and vegetables in a large stock pot; add remaining ingredients. Add more water, if necessary, to cover. Bring mixture to a boil; reduce heat and simmer 6 to 8 hours, skimming occasionally to remove any foam or impurities that rise to the top. Try not to let the mixture boil or the broth will be cloudy.

3. Strain into a container and cool to room temperature before refrigerating. (If hot stock is placed directly in the fridge, it will sometimes sour.) For a more intensely flavored stock, let liquid cool and remove any fat from the top; return stock to pot and, over low heat, simmer until volume is reduced by half.

To freeze: Let stock cool. Refrigerate. Discard congealed fat on surface. Ladle into freezer containers (2-cup [500 mL] or 4-cup [1 L] are good). Seal, label and date. Freeze for up to 4 months.

To serve: Thaw soup in microwave or in refrigerator overnight.

Basic Chicken Stock

**MAKES ABOUT
8 CUPS (2 L)**

The easiest of stocks to
make, this surpasses any
commercial variety because
you control the quality of
ingredients and the amount
of fat included. Salt may be
added when the stock is
used in a recipe. This
freezes well for up to
four months.

TIP

Freeze in quantities you
know you can use – 2-cup
(500 mL), 4-cup (1 L) or
6-cup (1.5 L) amounts.

Stocks freeze well for up to
3 months. When freezing
liquids, remember to leave
1-inch (2 cm) headspace
between stock and lid.

6	whole cloves	6
1	onion, peeled	1
2 1/2 lbs	chicken bones, backs, necks or wings	1 kg
1	carrot, chopped	1
1	stalk celery, chopped	1
4	sprigs fresh parsley	4
1	bay leaf	1
1/2 tsp	dried thyme leaves	2 mL
8 cups	cold water (approx)	2 L

1. Stick cloves in onion. Place in large stainless steel saucepan, along with chicken bones, carrot, celery, parsley, bay leaf and thyme. Add cold water to cover. Bring to a boil. Reduce heat; simmer, uncovered, for 1 to 1 1/2 hours, skimming any froth that rises to the surface.

2. Set fine mesh sieve over large container. Ladle stock into sieve, leaving behind dregs. Remove meat from bones and save for another use. Discard bones, vegetables and bay leaf.

To freeze: Let stock cool. Refrigerate. Discard congealed fat on surface. Ladle into freezer containers. Seal, label and date. Freeze for up to 4 months.

To serve: Thaw soup in microwave or in refrigerator overnight.

Basic Fish Stock

MAKES ABOUT 4 CUPS (1 L)

1 1/2 lbs	fish bones, including head and tail	750 g
4 cups	cold water	1 L
1 cup	dry white wine or juice of 1 lemon	250 mL
6	peppercorns	6
6	sprigs parsley	6
1	leek, chopped	1
1	stalk celery, chopped	1
1	bay leaf	1
1 tsp	leaf thyme	5 mL

Use bones, head and tail from lean white fish such as sole, haddock, plaice, flounder and lemon sole in this recipe. Avoid fatty fish such as salmon or mackerel which make the stock oily. Fish stock requires only a brief cooking of 20 minutes; otherwise, it will be bitter.

TIP

Use fish stock in recipes such as Easy Bouillabaisse, (see recipe, page 136).

1. In large stainless steel saucepan or Dutch oven, combine bones, water, wine, peppercorns, parsley, leek, celery, bay leaf and thyme. Bring to boil; reduce heat and simmer, uncovered, for 20 minutes, skimming surface if necessary.

2. Pour through sieve. Discard solids.

To freeze: Let stock cool. Refrigerate. Ladle into freezer containers. Seal, label and date. Freeze for up to 3 months.

To serve: Thaw stock in microwave or in refrigerator overnight.

Basic Vegetable Stock

**MAKES
4 CUPS (1 L)**

Use this stock in vegetarian soups and casseroles. For a richer flavor and color, brown the vegetables in 2 tbsp (25 mL) oil first.

4 cups	cold water	1 L
1	carrot, peeled and chopped	1
1	stalk celery, chopped	1
1	onion, chopped	1
1	leek, chopped	1
1	bay leaf	1
1 tsp	dried thyme	5 mL
6	peppercorns	6
6	sprigs parsley	6

1. In large stainless steel saucepan or Dutch oven, combine water, carrot, celery, onion, leek, bay leaf, thyme, peppercorns and parsley. Bring to boil; reduce heat and simmer, uncovered, for 1 hour. Strain through sieve. Discard solids.

To freeze: Let stock cool. Refrigerate. Ladle into freezer containers. Seal, label and date. Freeze for up to 3 months.

To serve: Thaw stock in microwave or in refrigerator overnight.

Basic Cooked Turkey Stock

After you've enjoyed a turkey meal, you have the makings of a delicious stock. If you don't feel like making stock immediately, simply break up the carcass, wrap in a freezer bag and freezer for up to four months. You can make the stock anytime within that period at your convenience. Please note, there is no salt in this recipe. It can be added when combined in a recipe.

6	whole cloves	6
1	onion, peeled	1
1	leftover cooked turkey carcass, broken into pieces	1
2	carrots, chopped	2
2	stalks celery, chopped	2
6	whole peppercorns	6
4	sprigs fresh parsley	4
1	bay leaf	1
1 tsp	dried thyme leaves	5 mL
	Cold water to cover carcass (about 12 cups [3 L])	

1. Stick cloves in onion. Place in large stainless steel saucepan, along with turkey carcass, carrot, celery, peppercorns, parsley, bay leaf and thyme. Add water to cover. Bring to a boil. Reduce heat; simmer, uncovered, for 1 1/2 hours, skimming any froth that rises to the surface.

2. Set fine mesh sieve over large container. Ladle stock into sieve, leaving behind dregs. Remove meat from carcass and save for another use. Discard bones, vegetables and bay leaf.

To freeze: Let stock cool. Refrigerate. Discard congealed fat on surface. Ladle into freezer containers. Seal, label and date. Freeze for up to 4 months.

To serve: Thaw stock in microwave or in refrigerator overnight.

Hearty Turkey Soup

**MAKES ABOUT
12 CUPS (3 L)**

This warming soup is the
ultimate comfort food on a
cold winter's night.

TIP

Freeze for up to 1 month in
usable amounts in plastic
containers; seal, date and
label. Leave about 1 inch
(2 cm) headspace between
soup and lid.

12 cups	Basic Cooked Turkey Stock (see recipe, page 72)	3 L
2	carrots, chopped	2
2	stalks celery, chopped	2
2	leeks, chopped	2
1/2 cup	uncooked small pasta, rice or barley	125 mL
2 cups	chopped cooked turkey meat	500 mL
1/2 cup	chopped fresh parsley	125 mL
	Salt and freshly ground black pepper	

1. In a large saucepan, combine turkey stock, carrots, celery, onion and pasta. Bring to a boil. Reduce heat; simmer covered 20 minutes or until vegetables are tender.

2. Stir in turkey meat and parsley. Season to taste with salt and pepper. *Serve immediately or proceed with "to freeze" section, below.*

To freeze: Let soup cool. Ladle into freezer containers. Seal, label and date. Freeze for up to 1 month.

To serve: Thaw soup in microwave or in refrigerator overnight.

Quick Chicken Noodle Soup

Serves 4

This soothing and satisfying soup is made in minutes with chicken left from Sunday's roast.

From Rose Murray: *Quick Chicken*

Freezer Tip

This soup is super fast and easy to prepare using cooked chicken from your freezer. You can also freeze the finished soup. Although its texture won't be quite as good, it will taste great.

2 tbsp	butter	25 mL
1 cup	diced carrots	250 mL
4	green onions, sliced	4
5 cups	chicken broth	1.25 L
1	bay leaf	1
	Salt and pepper	
4 oz	very thin egg noodles	125 g
1 cup	diced cooked chicken	250 mL
1/2 cup	frozen peas	125 mL

1. In a large saucepan, melt the butter over medium heat. Add carrots and cook for 3 minutes. Stir in green onions. Gradually stir in broth. Add bay leaf and salt and pepper to taste. Bring to a boil; reduce heat, cover and simmer for 3 to 5 minutes or until the carrots are almost tender.

2. Return soup to a boil. Add noodles, chicken and peas; simmer, uncovered, for 3 to 5 minutes until chicken is heated through and noodles are tender. Remove bay leaf and season to taste.

To freeze: Let soup cool. Ladle into freezer containers. Seal, label and date. Freeze for up to 3 months.

To serve: Thaw soup in microwave or in refrigerator overnight.

Chicken Tortellini Soup with Peas

SERVES 4

Convenient ingredients like tortellini, frozen vegetables and cans of chicken broth turn Sunday's leftover chicken into a hearty meal in no time.

From Rose Murray: Quick Chicken

FREEZER TIP

This soup is super fast and easy to prepare using frozen cooked chicken, peas and tortellini from your freezer. You can also freeze the finished soup (before adding the Parmesan). Although its texture won't be quite as good, it will taste great.

3	cloves garlic, minced	3
8 oz	fresh or frozen cheese tortellini	250 g
2	cans (10 oz [284 mL]) chicken broth	2
1 cup	frozen peas	250 mL
1 cup	diced cooked chicken	250 mL
1/4 tsp	pepper	1 mL
2 tbsp	chopped green onions	25 mL
AFTER FREEZING/BEFORE SERVING		
1/4 cup	freshly grated Parmesan cheese	50 mL

1. In a large pot, bring 3 cups (750 mL) water and the garlic to a boil. Add the tortellini; return to a boil. Reduce heat to medium-high; cook, stirring occasionally, for 10 minutes if fresh or 15 minutes if frozen, or according to the package instructions.

2. Add chicken broth and peas; return to a boil and cook for 2 minutes. Add chicken; cook for 1 minute. Stir in pepper and green onions. *If freezing soup, see "to freeze" section below; otherwise proceed with Step 3.*

3. Serve sprinkled with Parmesan cheese.

To freeze: Let soup cool. Ladle into freezer containers. Seal, label and date. Freeze for up to 3 months.

To serve: Thaw soup in microwave or in refrigerator overnight. Heat in a saucepan until hot. Proceed with Step 3, above.

Quick Chunky Minestrone

SERVES 4

Canned chickpeas or beans add lots of texture and nutrients to this "whole meal" soup that makes good use of some of Sunday's leftover roast chicken. Don't let the rather long ingredient list put you off; the soup is quick and easy to make.

MAKE AHEAD

The soup can be made and refrigerated in an airtight container up to 2 days ahead or frozen for up to 3 months.

From Rose Murray: *Quick Chicken*

4	slices bacon, diced	4
2	celery stalks, sliced	2
1	onion, chopped	1
1	carrot, sliced	1
1	clove garlic, minced	1
1	can (19 oz [540 mL]) tomatoes	1
4 cups	chicken stock	1 L
1/4 tsp	crumbled dried sage	1 mL
1/4 tsp	thyme	1 mL
1	can (19 oz [540 mL]) chickpeas or white kidney or Romano beans, rinsed and drained	1
4 oz	cut fresh or frozen green beans	125 g
1 cup	chopped or shredded cooked chicken	250 mL
1/4 cup	macaroni or any small pasta	50 mL
	Salt and pepper	

AFTER FREEZING/BEFORE SERVING

1/4 cup	freshly grated Parmesan cheese	50 mL

1 In a large saucepan, cook bacon over medium heat until crisp; remove with a slotted spoon and set aside to drain on paper towels.

2. Pour off all but 1 tbsp (15 mL) drippings from the pan. Add celery, onion, carrot and garlic; cook, stirring occasionally, for 5 minutes. Add tomatoes, breaking up with the back of a spoon. Add chicken stock, sage and thyme; bring to a boil. Reduce heat, cover and simmer for 5 minutes.

3. Add chickpeas, beans, chicken and macaroni; cook for 8 to 10 minutes or until the macaroni is tender but firm. Return cooked bacon to the pan. Season with salt and pepper to taste. *If freezing soup, see "to freeze" section below; otherwise proceed with Step 4.*

4. Serve sprinkled with Parmesan cheese.

To freeze: Let soup cool. Ladle into freezer containers, leaving headspace. Seal, label and date. Freeze for up to 3 months.

To serve: Thaw soup in microwave or in refrigerator overnight. Heat in a saucepan until hot. Proceed with Step 4, above.

Fresh Tomato Dill Soup

1 tbsp	olive oil	15 mL
1 tsp	crushed garlic	5 mL
1	medium carrot, chopped	1
1	celery stalk, chopped	1
1 cup	chopped onion	250 mL
2 cups	chicken stock	500 mL
5 cups	chopped ripe tomatoes	1.25 L
3 tbsp	tomato paste	45 mL
2 tsp	granulated sugar	10 mL
3 tbsp	chopped fresh dill	45 mL

1. In large nonstick saucepan, heat oil; sauté garlic, carrot, celery and onion until softened, approximately 5 minutes.

2. Add stock, tomatoes and tomato paste; reduce heat, cover and simmer for 20 minutes, stirring occasionally.

3. Purée in food processor until smooth. Add sugar and dill; mix well.

To freeze: Let soup cool. Ladle into freezer containers. Seal, label and date. Freeze for up to 3 months.

To serve: Thaw soup in microwave or in refrigerator overnight.

Hearty Tomato Vegetable Soup

SERVES 4 TO 6

This is a wonderful all-purpose soup. Serve with crusty bread for a complete meal or use as a base for a pasta topping or a hearty stew.

VARIATION

Hearty Tomato Vegetable Pasta Sauce: Add 2 tbsp (25 mL) all-purpose flour after step 1, stirring into softened vegetables until well combined. Gradually stir in remaining ingredients.

Hearty Tomato Vegetable Stew: Make Hearty Vegetable Pasta Sauce and add a can of drained, rinsed chickpeas.

1 tbsp	butter or vegetable oil	15 mL
2 cups	chopped onion, leeks and/or green onions	500 mL
2 cups	mushrooms	500 mL
1 cup	diced celery	250 mL
1 cup	coarsely chopped red or green bell pepper	250 mL
2	cloves garlic, minced	2
1	can (28 oz [796 mL]) diced tomatoes	1
1 cup	Basic Chicken Stock (see recipe, page 69)	250 mL
1	bay leaf	1
2 tsp	granulated sugar	10 mL
1 tsp	dried basil	5 mL
1 tsp	dried thyme leaves	5 mL
1/2 tsp	dried rosemary leaves	2 mL
1/4 tsp	salt	1 mL
1/4 tsp	freshly ground black pepper	1 mL

AFTER FREEZING/BEFORE SERVING

1/2 cup	sour cream or yogurt	125 mL
1/4 cup	minced fresh parsley	50 mL

1. In a large saucepan, melt butter over medium-high heat. Stir in onions, mushrooms, celery, peppers and garlic; cover and cook for 5 minutes or until onions are softened.

2. Stir in tomatoes and juice, chicken stock, bay leaf, sugar, basil, thyme, rosemary, salt and pepper. Bring to a boil. Reduce heat; simmer, covered, for 15 to 20 minutes. *If freezing soup, see "to freeze" section below; otherwise proceed with Step 3.*

3. In small bowl, stir together sour cream and parsley; garnish each bowl of soup with a large dollop of mixture, swirling through soup.

To freeze: Let soup cool. Ladle into freezer containers. Seal, label and date. Freeze for up to 4 months.

To serve: Thaw soup in microwave or in refrigerator overnight. Heat in a saucepan until hot. Proceed with Step 3, above.

Curried Parsnip and Pear Soup

**MAKES ABOUT 8
CUPS (2 L)**

This soup makes a
wonderful accompaniment
to pork or poultry dishes. It
is also an amazingly
versatile recipe – you can
make it with practically any
vegetable or combination
of vegetables you wish,
and season it with a variety
of different herbs to create
a whole range of flavor
combinations. It is excellent
served hot in the winter
and chilled in the summer.
Because vegetables thicken
the soup, it is low in fat,
making it ideal for those
trying to lose weight and
incorporate more
vegetables into their diet.
Kids also love this soup!

1 lb	parsnips, chopped	500 g
1 lb	carrots, chopped	500 g
1	onion, chopped	1
1	stalk celery, chopped	1
1	pear, peeled and chopped	1
6 cups	Basic Chicken Stock (see recipe, page 69)	1.5 L
1	bay leaf	1
1	can (14 oz [385 L]) evaporated milk	1
1 tsp	salt	5 mL
1 tsp	curry powder	5 mL
1/2 tsp	freshly ground black pepper	2 mL
1/2 tsp	freshly grated nutmeg	2 mL

AFTER FREEZING/BEFORE SERVING

Chopped fresh coriander or parsley

1. In a large saucepan, combine parsnips, carrots, onion, celery, pear, chicken stock and bay leaf. Bring to a boil. Reduce heat; simmer, covered, for 25 to 30 minutes or until vegetables are very tender.

2. Discard bay leaf. Stir in evaporated milk, salt, curry, pepper and nutmeg. In batches, purée in blender or food processor until smooth. *If freezing soup, see "to freeze" section below; otherwise proceed with Step 3.*

3. Serve garnished with coriander or parsley.

To freeze: Let soup cool. Ladle into freezer containers. Seal, label and date. Freeze for up to 4 months.

To serve: Thaw soup in microwave or in refrigerator overnight. Heat in a saucepan until hot. Proceed with Step 3, above.

Broccoli Soup with Tarragon

SERVES 4 TO 6

This is a soothing soup, made speedily with that ever-present vegetable, broccoli.

1	bunch broccoli, coarsely chopped	1
1	large onion, coarsely chopped	1
1	large potato, peeled and coarsely chopped	1
3 cups	Basic Chicken Stock (see recipe, page 69)	750 mL
2 tsp	dried tarragon	10 mL
1	bay leaf	1
1 tsp	salt	5 mL
1/4 tsp	freshly ground black pepper	1 mL
AFTER FREEZING/BEFORE SERVING		
1 cup	yogurt or evaporated milk or sour cream	250 mL
1/2 cup	crumbled blue cheese or shredded old Cheddar cheese	125 mL

1. In a large saucepan, combine broccoli, onion potato, stock , tarragon, bay leaf, salt and pepper. Bring to a boil. Reduce heat; simmer, covered, for 25 minutes or until vegetables are very tender. Discard bay leaf.

2. In batches, purée in blender or food processor until smooth. *If freezing soup, see "to freeze" section below; otherwise proceed with Step 3.*

3. Stir in yogurt. Garnish soup with cheese, swirling it into the hot soup.

To freeze: Let soup cool. Ladle into freezer containers. Seal, label and date. Freeze for up to 4 months.

To serve: Thaw soup in microwave or in refrigerator overnight. Heat in a saucepan until hot. Proceed with Step 3, above.

Ratatouille

MAKES ABOUT 8 CUPS (2 L)

This versatile dish can be served hot as a vegetable or cold as a salad. It can also be used as an appetizer, a pasta sauce, or a companion to a roast.

1/4 cup	olive oil	50 mL
1 1/2 cups	diced onions	375 mL
2	cloves garlic, minced	2
1	eggplant, skin on, cut into 1/2-inch (1 cm) cubes	1
3	zucchini, skin on, sliced 1/4 inch (5 mm) thick	3
1	red bell pepper, chopped	1
1	green pepper, chopped	1
1 tbsp	granulated sugar	15 mL
1 tbsp	dried basil	15 mL
1 tsp	dried oregano	5 mL
1	can (28 oz [796 mL]) diced tomatoes	1
1/2 cup	chopped fresh parsley	125 mL
	Salt and freshly ground black pepper	

1. In a large saucepan, heat oil over medium high heat. Add onions and garlic; cook 5 minutes or until softened.

2. Stir in eggplant, zucchini, peppers, sugar, basil, oregano, tomatoes and juices. Bring to a boil. Reduce heat; cover and simmer for 20 to 30 minutes. Stir in parsley. Season to taste with salt and pepper.

To freeze: Let mixture cool. Ladle into freezer containers. Seal, label and date. Freeze for up to 4 months.

To serve: Thaw stew in microwave or in refrigerator overnight.

Chicken Salad Niçoise

SERVES 6

The classic version of this salad is made with tuna, but chicken makes a light, delicious variation for a hot summer day. Plan the night before to cook extra potatoes and beans. Don't let the long ingredient list put you off; the salad is quick and easy to make.

MAKE AHEAD

The dressing can be made up to 1 day ahead and refrigerated. Bring to room temperature and whisk to recombine before using. The salad ingredients can be tossed together (end of step 2) several hours ahead and refrigerated.

From Rose Murray: *Quick Chicken*

GARLIC DRESSING

2	cloves garlic, crushed	2
2 tsp	Dijon mustard	10 mL
1/4 cup	fresh lemon juice	50 mL
1/2 cup	olive oil	125 mL
	Salt and pepper	

SALAD

2 cups	shredded cooked chicken	500 mL
2 cups	cooked green beans, cut into 2-inch (5 cm) lengths	500 mL
6	small new potatoes, cooked and sliced	6
1	small red bell pepper, cut into strips	1
1	small red onion, thinly sliced	1
2 cups	sliced celery	500 mL
3/4 cup	black olives	175 mL
	Romaine lettuce, torn into bite-sized pieces	
3	hard-cooked eggs, quartered	3
4	tomatoes, cut into wedges	4

1. Garlic Dressing: In a small bowl, whisk together garlic, mustard and lemon juice. Gradually whisk in oil. Season to taste with salt and pepper. Set aside.

2. In a large bowl, combine chicken, beans, potatoes, red pepper, onion, celery and olives.

3. Pour dressing over chicken mixture and gently toss to coat. Line a shallow salad bowl with lettuce and spoon salad on top. Garnish with eggs and tomatoes.

FREEZER TIP

It would be great if you could freeze a salad and have it ready to go at a moment's notice. Unfortunately salads and freezers don't mix. But that doesn't mean you can't speed up the preparation of a salad like this one – using ingredients from your freezer such as cooked chicken, green beans and bell peppers. Try it!

Salmon or Tuna Sandwich Filling

**MAKES ABOUT
1 1/4 CUPS
(300 mL),**
ENOUGH FOR ABOUT 4
SANDWICHES

VARIATION

CHICKEN SALAD SANDWICH
Filling: Use 1 cup (250 mL)
cooked chopped chicken
instead of the fish and
substitute chopped
tarragon for the dill

HAM SALAD SANDWICH
Filling: Use 1 cup (250 mL)
diced Black Forest ham
instead of the fish and
substitute chopped parsley
for the dill.

1	can salmon (7 1/2 oz [213 g]) or tuna (6 oz [170 g]), drained	1
4 oz	cream cheese, softened	125 g
2 tbsp	whipped salad dressing	25 mL
2 tbsp	finely chopped green onions	25 mL
2 tbsp	finely chopped fresh dill	25 mL
2 tbsp	fresh lemon juice	25 mL
1/4 tsp	freshly ground black pepper	1 mL

1. If using salmon, discard skin.

2. Place fish, including salmon bones (if using salmon) in food processor, along with cream cheese, salad dressing, green onions, dill, lemon juice and pepper. Pulse on and off until well mixed. Spread on well-buttered bread to make sandwiches.

To freeze: Wrap in freezer bags. Seal, label and date. Freeze for up to 6 weeks.

To serve: Thaw in refrigerator overnight. Or pack frozen in lunch bag in the morning; eat at noon, when thawed.

Hawaiian Tuna Wraps

MAKES 6 WRAPS

Use whole wheat or flavored tortillas for a twist.

1	can (6 oz [170 g]) water-packed chunk light tuna, drained	1
4 oz	cream cheese, softened	125 g
3/4 cup	drained crushed pineapple	175 mL
1/4 cup	salted sunflower seeds	50 mL
1 tbsp	chopped fresh parsley	15 mL
1/2 tsp	curry powder	2 mL
6	small tortillas	6

1. In a bowl using electric mixer, combine tuna, cream cheese, pineapple, sunflower seeds, parsley and curry powder; mix until well blended.

2. Spoon about 1/3 cup (75 mL) filling onto each tortilla. Roll up.

To freeze: Wrap well with plastic wrap, overwrap in heavy foil. Freeze for up to 6 weeks.

To serve: Thaw in refrigerator overnight. Or pack frozen in lunch bag in the morning; eat at noon, when thawed.

Cornish Pasty

PREHEAT OVEN TO 425° F (230° C)

MAKES 4 PIES

Prepared pastry makes light work of these pocket-sized meat pies – at one time the traditional lunch of English miners.

TIP

Instead of freezing from baked, wrap well after Step 2 and freeze unbaked for up to 1 month; omit egg wash. Bake from frozen in 400° F (200° C) oven for 25 minutes or until golden.

FILLING

8 oz	lean ground beef	250 g
1/3 cup	grated carrot	75 mL
1/3 cup	chopped potato	75 mL
1/3 cup	chopped onion	75 mL
3/4 cup	water	175 mL
2 tbsp	ketchup	25 mL
1 tsp	Worcestershire sauce	5 mL
1/2 tsp	salt	2 mL
1/4 tsp	freshly ground black pepper	1 mL
2	9-inch (23 cm) prepared pastry shells, thawed	2
1	egg	1
1 tbsp	water	15 mL

1. Filling: In a frying pan, cook beef, carrot, potato, and onion over medium high heat 8 to 10 minutes or until onion is softened and beef is no longer pink. Stir in water, ketchup and Worcestershire. Continue to cook covered 5 to 7 minutes or until potato is tender. Stir in salt and pepper. Cool.

2. Meanwhile, invert each pie shell onto a piece of waxed paper, discarding foil liner. Gently flatten pastry shell and reshape if necessary. Cut each shell in half. Spoon one-quarter of filling onto bottom half of each piece of pastry. Fold pastry in half to enclose filling. Crimp edges together firmly. Transfer to baking sheet. Cut one or two vents in each pie.

3. In small bowl, beat egg with water; brush over pies. Bake in center of oven for 15 to 20 minutes or until golden.

To freeze: Let pasties cool. Wrap well with plastic wrap, then overwrap in heavy foil. Freeze for up to 2 months.

To serve: Thaw in refrigerator overnight. Or pack frozen in lunch bag in the morning; eat at noon, when thawed. May be eaten cold or hot. To re-heat, bake thawed, uncovered pasties on baking sheet at 350° F (180° C) for about 20 minutes or until heated through.

Ground Chicken Pizza

PREHEAT OVEN TO 500° F (260° C)

SERVES 3 OR 4

This easy pizza has lots of kid appeal. For pineapple aficionados, top the chicken with pineapple tidbits before sprinkling on the last of the cheese.

SHOPPING TIP

Pizza dough is quite often available in the freezer section of supermarkets. Pre-made uncooked crusts can be found in the cooler section where there are store-made pizzas. Or, stop by your local pizzeria and buy 1 lb (500 g) dough for a crust.

From Rose Murray: *Quick Chicken*

2 tbsp	olive oil	25 mL
12 oz	lean ground chicken	375 g
8 oz	mushrooms, sliced	250 g
Half	green pepper, in chunks	Half
1	12-inch (30 cm) uncooked pizza crust or 1 lb (500 g) pizza dough	1
8 oz	mozzarella or provolone cheese, shredded	250 g
1 tsp	dried Italian herb seasoning	5 mL
1	can (7 1/2 oz [213 mL]) pizza sauce	1

1. In a large skillet, heat half the oil over medium-high heat. Add chicken and cook for 5 minutes, breaking it up with a spoon. Add mushrooms and cook for 5 minutes. Add green pepper and cook for 1 minute.

2. Brush pizza crust with some of the remaining oil; sprinkle with half the cheese. Stir herb seasoning into the sauce; spread over top of the cheese. Arrange chicken mixture on top and sprinkle with remaining cheese. Drizzle with remaining oil. Bake pizza in preheated oven for 12 to 15 minutes or until crust is golden brown.

To freeze: Let pizza cool. Wrap well with plastic wrap, then over-wrap in heavy foil. Freeze for up to 6 weeks.

To serve: Thaw in refrigerator overnight. To re-heat, bake thawed, uncovered pizza on baking sheet at 350° F (180° C) for about 20 minutes or until heated through.

Muffeletta

**Makes 4
sandwiches**

A giant-sized sandwich with giant Italian flavors – great for the workplace as well as a school lunch.

4	panini buns	4
3/4 cup	pesto (see recipe, page 54)	175 mL
1 cup	grated Parmesan cheese	250 mL
1	jar 16 oz [500 mL]) roasted red peppers, drained and sliced	1
1	jar (6 oz [170 mL]) marinated artichokes, drained and chopped	1
4 oz	thinly sliced smoked ham or Italian salami	125 g

1. Cut buns horizontally, three-quarters of the way through. Spread each cut side generously with pesto. On bottom halves, divide cheese, red peppers, artichokes and ham. Press rolls firmly together.

To freeze: Wrap well with plastic wrap, then place in large freezer bag. Freeze for up to 6 weeks.

To serve: Thaw in refrigerator overnight. Or pack frozen in lunch bag in the morning; eat at noon, when thawed.

Chicken Frittata

PREHEAT BROILER

SERVES 3 OR 4

My good friend and able assistant, Sharon Boyd, often makes a frittata for her family using whatever is at hand in her refrigerator. Feel free to use whatever you want in this easy supper dish. Add a small sliced zucchini or some chopped broccoli with the pepper; or substitute corn for the peas; add some sliced cooked potatoes with the chicken. It's also a good way to use up ends of cheese; Fontina, Cheddar or provolone are all good melting cheeses.

From Rose Murray: Quick Chicken

6	eggs	6
1/2 tsp	salt	2 mL
1/4 tsp	pepper	1 mL
1/4 tsp	dried thyme	1 mL
1/4 tsp	oregano	1 mL
1 tbsp	butter	15 mL
1 tbsp	vegetable oil	15 mL
1	onion, chopped	1
1	small red bell pepper, diced	1
1 cup	diced cooked chicken	250 mL
1 cup	frozen peas	250 mL
1 1/2 cups	shredded Swiss cheese	375 mL

1. In a bowl whisk together eggs, salt, pepper, thyme and oregano. Set aside.

2. In a large ovenproof skillet, melt butter with oil over medium heat. Add onion and red pepper; cook for about 5 minutes until softened. Stir in chicken and peas; spread out in pan. Pour egg mixture on top. Cook for 7 to 10 minutes, tilting pan occasionally and pulling mixture from sides with a spatula, until eggs start to set around the edge but center still jiggles slightly.

3. Sprinkle with cheese. Place skillet about 5 inches (12.5 cm) from heat and broil 3 minutes or until golden brown and set. Cut in wedges to serve.

FREEZER TIP

Here's a speedy brunch/lunch dish which, although it can't be frozen after cooking, is much easier to prepare when you use ingredients from your freezer such as cooked chicken, peas and bell peppers.

Taco Pitas

SERVES 4

Ever since I devised these yummy tacos, I walk right on by the prepackaged taco mixes and shells in supermarkets. Once the meat is browned, it takes no time to add the beans and seasonings to make the tasty filling. Aside from being lower in fat, I find pita breads make much better containers than taco shells, which tend to crumble when you bite into them and cause the filling to spill out.

Double the recipe and freeze extras for another meal.

The only major chore left to getting supper ready is shredding the cheese and preparing the vegetable garnishes – simple tasks that young cooks can handle.

TIP

To heat pitas, wrap in foil and place in a 350° F (180° C) oven for 15 to 20 minutes. Or wrap 4 at a time in paper towels and microwave at High for 1 to 1 1/2 minutes.

VARIATION

Sloppy Joe Pitas: Increase beef to 1 lb (500 g). Omit beans and add 1 can (7 1/2 oz [213 mL]) tomato sauce; cook 3 minutes more or until sauce is slightly thickened.

From Johanna Burkhard: *The Comfort Food Cookbook*

8 oz	lean ground beef	250 g
1	small onion, finely chopped	1
1	large garlic clove, minced	1
2 tsp	chili powder	10 mL
2 tsp	all-purpose flour	10 mL
1/2 tsp	dried oregano	2 mL
1/2 tsp	ground cumin	2 mL
Pinch	cayenne pepper	Pinch
1/2 cup	beef stock	125 mL
1	can (19 oz [540 mL]) pinto, black or red kidney beans, rinsed and drained	1

AFTER FREEZING/BEFORE SERVING

6	pitas (7-inch [18 cm] size), halved to form pockets, warmed	6
	Salsa, shredded lettuce, tomato wedges, pepper strips, shredded mozzarella or cheddar cheese	

1. In a large nonstick skillet over medium-high heat, cook beef, breaking up with the back of a spoon, for 4 minutes or until no longer pink.

2. Reduce heat to medium. Add onion, garlic, chili powder, flour, oregano, cumin and cayenne pepper. Cook, stirring often, for 5 minutes or until onions are softened.

3. Pour in stock; cook, stirring, until slightly thickened. Stir in beans; cook 2 minutes more or until heated through. *If freezing, see "to freeze" section below; otherwise proceed with Step 4.*

4. Spoon 1/4 cup (50 mL) of the mixture into pita pockets; top with salsa, lettuce, tomato, pepper and cheese.

To freeze: Let filling mixture cool. Ladle into freezer containers. Seal, label and date. Freeze for up to 3 months.

To serve: Thaw filling in microwave or in refrigerator overnight. Heat in a saucepan until warmed through. Proceed with Step 4, above.

Meatloaf 'Muffins' with Barbecue Sauce

PREHEAT OVEN TO 375° F (190° C)
12-CUP MUFFIN TIN, GREASED

SERVES 6

TIP

If your kids don't like onion pieces in the sauce, substitute 1/4 tsp (1 mL) onion or garlic powder. Limit use of onion or garlic salt, as they add unnecessary sodium.

FOOD FAST

Instead of making the sauce, substitute 1 cup (250 mL) of your favorite prepared barbecue sauce.

NUTRITION FACTS

Adding wheat bran is a great way to boost the fiber content of meatloaf and hamburgers. Canned evaporated milk or skim milk powder helps increase calcium.

From Dietitians of Canada: *Great Food Fast*

MEATLOAF "MUFFINS"

1 1/2 lbs	lean ground beef	750 g
3/4 cup	oatmeal or dry bread crumbs or cracker crumbs	175 mL
1/4 cup	wheat bran	50 mL
1	can (5.4 oz [160 mL]) evaporated 2% milk	1
1	egg	1
1 tsp	chili powder	5 mL
1/2 tsp	garlic powder	2 mL
1/4 tsp	salt	1 mL
1/4 tsp	black pepper	1 mL

BARBECUE SAUCE

1 cup	ketchup	250 mL
1/4 cup	finely chopped onion	50 mL
2 tbsp	brown sugar	25 mL
1/2 tsp	hot pepper sauce (optional)	2 mL

1. Muffins: In a large bowl, combine ground beef, oatmeal, bran, milk, egg, chili powder, garlic powder, salt and pepper. Divide mixture evenly among muffin cups, pressing down lightly.

2. Sauce: In another bowl, combine ketchup, onion, sugar and, if using, hot pepper sauce. Spoon about 1 tbsp (15 mL) sauce over each muffin.

3. Bake in preheated oven for 25 to 30 minutes or until meat is no longer pink in center.

To freeze: Wrap in freezer bags. Seal, label and date. Freeze for up to 2 months.

To serve: Thaw in microwave or in refrigerator overnight. Reheat thawed "muffins" in baking disk at 350° F (180° C) for about 20 minutes or until heated through.

Best-Ever Meat Loaf

PREHEAT OVEN TO 350° F (180° C)
9- BY 5-INCH (2 L) LOAF PAN

SERVES 6

I could make this juicy meat loaf with garlic mashed potatoes every week and never hear a complaint from my family that it's served too often.

TIP

I like to use oatmeal as a binder, since it gives a coarser texture to the meat loaf (bread crumbs produce a finer one). Use whichever binder you prefer.

I always double the recipe and wrap the extra cooked meat loaf in plastic wrap, then in foil, for the freezer. Defrost overnight in the fridge. To reheat, cut into slices and place in saucepan. Moisten with about 1/2 cup (125 mL) beef stock; set over medium heat until piping hot. Or place meat loaf and stock in casserole dish and microwave at Medium until heated through.

From Johanna Burkhard: *The Comfort Food Cookbook*

1 tbsp	vegetable oil	15 mL
1	medium onion, chopped	1
2	cloves garlic, minced	2
1 tsp	dried basil	5 mL
1 tsp	dried marjoram	5 mL
3/4 tsp	salt	4 mL
1/4 tsp	pepper	1 mL
1	egg	1
1/4 cup	chili sauce or ketchup	50 mL
1 tbsp	Worcestershire sauce	15 mL
2 tbsp	chopped fresh parsley	25 mL
1 1/2 lbs	lean ground beef	750 g
3/4 cup	rolled oats	175 mL
	or	
1/2 cup	dry bread crumbs	125 mL

1. In a large nonstick skillet, heat oil over medium heat. Add onion, garlic, basil, marjoram, salt and pepper; cook, stirring, for 3 minutes or until softened. (Or place in microwave-safe bowl; microwave, covered, at High for 3 minutes.) Let cool slightly.

2. In a large bowl, beat the egg; stir in onion mixture, chili sauce, Worcestershire sauce and parsley. Crumble beef over mixture and sprinkle with rolled oats. Using a wooden spoon or with your hands, gently mix until evenly combined.

3. Pack meat mixture lightly into loaf pan. Bake in preheated oven for 1 hour or until meat thermometer registers 170° F (75° C). Let stand for 5 minutes; drain fat in pan and turn out onto a plate. *If freezing, see "to freeze" section below; otherwise proceed with Step 4.*

4. Cut into thick slices and serve.

To freeze: Let meatloaf cool. Wrap well with plastic wrap, then overwrap in heavy foil. Freeze for up to 2 months.

To serve: See thawing/serving instructions in Tip, at left.

Baked Ham Fondue

SIX 3/4-CUP (175 mL) RAMEKINS OR CUSTARD CUPS,
SPRAYED WITH BAKING SPRAY

SERVES 6

A simplified version of a soufflé, this fondue can be assembled and frozen ahead, ready to pop into the oven. Serve with a salad for brunch or supper.

VARIATION

Baked Salmon or Tuna Fondue: Use 2 cans (each 7 1/2 oz [213 g]) salmon or tuna instead of ham, discarding salmon skin. Use Cheddar instead of Swiss.

2	eggs	2
1 1/2 cups	milk	375 mL
1 tbsp	whipped salad dressing	15 mL
1 1/2 tsp	Dijon mustard	7 mL
1/4 tsp	freshly ground black pepper	1 mL
3 cups	1/2-inch (1 cm) cubes day-old bread	750 mL
1 cup	chopped Black Forest ham	250 mL
1 cup	shredded Swiss cheese or old Cheddar cheese	250 mL

1. In a bowl whisk together eggs, milk, salad dressing, mustard and pepper. Stir in bread cubes. Let stand 10 minutes.

2. In another bowl, stir together ham and 3/4 cup (175 mL) of the cheese.

3. Stir ham mixture into bread mixture, combing well. Spoon into prepared dish. Sprinkle with remaining cheese. *If freezing, see "to freeze" section below; otherwise proceed with Step 4.*

4. Preheat oven to 350° F (180° C). Bake about 20 minutes or until puffed, and egg has set. Let stand several minutes before serving.

To freeze: Cover well with plastic wrap, then overwrap with foil. Freeze for up to 1 month.

To serve: Can be cooked from frozen. Proceed with Step 3, increasing baking time to 35 minutes.

Chicken Shepherd's Pie

Serves 4

Cook extra potatoes the night before you prepare this lean, delicious version of an old favorite. Or boil peeled, quartered potatoes while the chicken cooks. And if you have leftover vegetables, you can also chop them to use instead of the frozen variety.

Make Ahead

Both the chicken mixture and potato topping can be made ahead, covered and refrigerated up to 1 day. Bring chicken to a simmer before proceeding. Or complete the whole pie, cover and refrigerate. Warm gently to a simmer, then broil.

From Rose Murray: Quick Chicken

1 tsp	vegetable oil	5 mL
1	onion, chopped	1
1	clove garlic, chopped	1
1 lb	ground chicken	500 g
1 tbsp	all-purpose flour	15 mL
1 cup	chicken stock	250 mL
2 cups	frozen mixed vegetables	500 mL
1 tbsp	ketchup	15 mL
1 tbsp	Worcestershire sauce	15 mL
1/2 tsp	dried sage	2 mL
1/2 tsp	dried thyme	2 mL
	Salt and pepper	
4 oz	light cream cheese, softened	125 g
1	egg	1
4 cups	mashed potatoes	1 L

1. In a deep 10-inch (25 cm) ovenproof skillet, heat oil over medium heat. Add onion and garlic; cook for 3 minutes or until soft. Add chicken; cook, breaking up with the back of a spoon, for 5 to 7 minutes or until no longer pink. Sprinkle with flour; cook, stirring, for 1 minute. Gradually stir in stock; raise heat and cook, stirring, until thickened.

2. Stir in vegetables, ketchup, Worcestershire sauce, sage and thyme; bring to a boil. Reduce heat and simmer uncovered for 5 minutes. Season with salt and pepper to taste.

3. Meanwhile, beat cheese and egg into potatoes. Season with salt and pepper to taste. Spoon over chicken mixture. Place pan (covering handle with foil if not ovenproof) in the bottom third of the oven and broil for 7 to 8 minutes or until potatoes are heated through and golden brown.

To freeze: Let pie cool. Wrap well with plastic wrap, then overwrap with heavy foil. Seal, label and date. Freeze for up to 3 months.

To serve: Thaw in microwave or in refrigerator overnight. Preheat oven to 350° F (180° C). Unwrap baking dish. Bake for 20 minutes or until heated through.

Vegetarian Shepherd's Pie with Peppered Potato Topping

PREHEAT OVEN TO 350° F (180° C)
13- BY 9-INCH (3 L) BAKING DISH

SERVES 6 TO 8

TIP

This shepherd's pie rivals the beef version – creamy, thick and rich tasting. Beans provide the meat-like texture.

For a different twist, try sweet potatoes.

Try other cheeses such as mozzarella or Swiss.

MAKE AHEAD

Prepare up to 1 day in advance. Reheat gently.

Freeze for up to 3 weeks.

2 tsp	vegetable oil	10 mL
2 tsp	minced garlic	10 mL
1 cup	chopped onions	250 mL
3/4 cup	finely chopped carrots	175 mL
1 1/2 cups	prepared tomato pasta sauce	375 mL
1 cup	canned red kidney beans, rinsed and drained	250 mL
1 cup	canned chickpeas, rinsed and drained	250 mL
1/2 cup	Basic Vegetable Stock (see recipe, page 36) or water	125 mL
1 1/2 tsp	dried basil	7 mL
2	bay leaves	2
4 cups	diced potatoes	1 L
1/2 cup	2% milk	125 mL
1/3 cup	light sour cream	75 mL
1/4 tsp	freshly ground black pepper	1 mL
3/4 cup	shredded Cheddar cheese	175 mL
3 tbsp	grated Parmesan cheese	45 mL

1. In a saucepan heat oil over medium-high heat. Add garlic, onions and carrots; cook 4 minutes or until onion is softened. Stir in tomato sauce, kidney beans, chickpeas, stock, basil and bay leaves; reduce heat to medium-low, cover and cook 15 minutes or until vegetables are tender. Remove bay leaves. Transfer sauce to a food processor; pulse on and off just until chunky. Spread over bottom of baking dish.

2. Place potatoes in a saucepan; add cold water to cover. Bring to a boil, reduce heat and simmer 10 to 12 minutes or until tender. Drain; mash with milk, sour cream and pepper. Spoon on top of sauce in baking dish. Sprinkle with cheeses.

3. Bake, uncovered, 20 minutes or until hot.

To freeze: Let pie cool. Wrap well with plastic wrap, then heavy foil. Seal, label and date. Freeze for up to 3 months.

To serve: Thaw in microwave or in refrigerator overnight. Preheat oven to 350° F (180° C). Unwrap baking dish. Bake for 20 minutes or until heated through.

Pork and Chickpea Casserole

SERVES 4 TO 6

A hearty casserole ideal for wintry days. Serve with a dollop of yogurt or sour cream, crusty bread and a salad.

TIP

Be sure to pack in a tightly sealed container to avoid moisture loss. While reheating, stir in a little extra water.

8 oz	Italian sausages (sweet or hot)	250 g
2 tbsp	vegetable oil	25 mL
1 1/2 lbs	boneless pork butt cut into 1-inch (2.5 cm) cubes	750 g
1 cup	chopped onions	250 mL
2	cloves garlic, minced	2
1	can (28 oz [796 mL]) diced tomatoes	1
1	can (19 oz [540 mL]) chickpeas, rinsed and drained	1
1 cup	water or white wine	250 mL
1/2 cup	rice (preferably brown)	125 mL
2 tsp	dried basil	10 mL
1 tsp	Worcestershire sauce	5 mL
	Salt and freshly ground black pepper	
1/2 cup	finely chopped fresh parsley	125 mL

1. In a saucepan arrange sausages in a single layer. Pour in about 1/2 inch (1 cm) water and bring to a boil. Reduce heat to simmer; cook about 10 minutes or until sausages are no longer pink inside. Drain and cool. Cut sausages into 1-inch (2.5 cm) slices.

2. In a large saucepan, heat oil over medium high heat. In batches, brown pork.

3. Return all pork to saucepan. Stir in onions and garlic; cook for 5 minutes or until onions are softened. Stir in sausages, tomatoes and juices, chickpeas, water, rice, basil and Worcestershire sauce. Bring to a boil. Reduce heat; simmer, covered, for 30 to 35 minutes or until rice and pork are tender. Remove bay leaf. Season to taste with salt and pepper. Stir in parsley.

To freeze: Let casserole cool. Spoon into freezer containers; seal, date and label. Freeze for up to 2 months.

To serve: Thaw in microwave or in refrigerator overnight. Preheat oven to 350° F (180° C). Transfer from freezer container(s) to baking dish. Bake for 20 minutes or until heated through.

CHICKEN SALAD NIÇOISE (PAGE 83) ➤
OVERLEAF: GROUND CHICKEN PIZZA (PAGE 87)

Lazy Lasagna

PREHEAT OVEN TO 350° F (180° C)
13- BY 9-INCH (3 L) BAKING DISH, GREASED

SERVES 8

Here's a quick way to get all the satisfying flavor and texture of lasagna without spending a lot of time in the kitchen. It's a perfect lunch-box treat — just heat it up in the microwave in the morning, pop into a short, wide-mouth thermos, pack with the rest of your lunch and off you go.

MAKE AHEAD

When you have time to cook, bake up two batches of this lasagna. Enjoy one batch for supper then divide the other into individual portions, freeze in airtight containers and use as needed for meals or lunches. If planning to freeze, use fresh (not previously frozen) ground beef.

From Dietitians of Canada: *Great Food Fast*

3 cups	penne, rotini or other large pasta	750 mL
2 tsp	olive oil	10 mL
12 oz	lean ground beef	375 g
1/2 cup	chopped onions	125 mL
1 cup	finely chopped or grated carrots	250 mL
1	jar (24 to 25 oz [700 to 750 mL]) prepared tomato pasta sauce	1
1/2 tsp	Italian seasoning *or* dried oregano or basil	2 mL
1	container (17 oz [475 g]) light ricotta cheese	1
1	egg	1
1 1/2 cups	grated partly skimmed mozzarella cheese	375 mL
1/4 cup	grated Parmesan cheese	50 mL

1. In a large pot of boiling water, cook pasta until tender but firm; drain. Toss with olive oil; set aside.

2. In a large skillet, cook beef over medium-high heat until browned. Add onions and carrots; cook for 3 to 4 minutes. Stir in pasta sauce and Italian seasoning. Remove from heat and set aside.

3. In a bowl combine ricotta cheese, egg and 1 cup (250 mL) of the mozzarella cheese. Set aside.

4. To assemble: Spread half of the meat mixture on bottom of baking dish. Top with all of the pasta. Spread all of the cheese mixture over pasta. Top with remaining meat mixture. Sprinkle with remaining 1/2 cup (125 mL) mozzarella cheese and Parmesan cheese.

5. Bake in preheated oven, uncovered, for 35 to 45 minutes or until bubbling and brown on top. Let stand for 10 minutes before serving.

To freeze: Let lasgana cool. Wrap well with plastic wrap, then heavy foil. Seal, label and date. Freeze for up to 3 months.

To serve: Thaw in microwave or in refrigerator overnight. Preheat oven to 350° F (180° C). Unwrap baking dish. Bake in center of oven for 25 minutes or until heated through.

◄ CHICKEN CHILI MACARONI (PAGE 104)

Chicken Tetrazzini

PREHEAT OVEN TO 375° F (190° C)
13- BY 9-INCH (3 L) BAKING DISH.

SERVES 8

This crowd-pleasing, old-fashioned casserole never goes out of style, especially because it is ideal for buffets and freezes well. Remember to allow a full 24 hours for casseroles to thaw in the refrigerator.

TIP

If freezing, undercook the pasta just until firm; it will cook further in the juicy sauce upon reheating. If making to serve immediately, cook pasta a little further.

Breadcrumb toppings become soggy on freezing. To crisp them, be sure to bake uncovered for at least 20 minutes or until golden brown and crisp.

Because casseroles dry out when freezing make sure sauces are thin before freezing. They will thicken once they are cooked.

OVEN-POACHED CHICKEN

1	4-lb (2 kg) roasting chicken	1
2 cups	chicken stock or water	500 mL
1 cup	dry white wine	250 mL
1	bay leaf	1
1 tsp	dried tarragon	5 mL
1 tsp	dried thyme leaves	5 mL

TETRAZZINI

1	pkg (12 oz/375 g) broad egg noodles	1
1/3 cup	butter	75 mL
1 1/2 cups	chopped onions	375 mL
1 cup	chopped celery	250 mL
1 cup	chopped green peppers	250 mL
2	cloves garlic, minced	2
2 cups	sliced mushrooms	500 mL
1/4 cup	all-purpose flour	50 mL
3 cups	reserved chicken stock	750 mL
1 cup	light (10%) cream	250 mL
1/4 cup	dry sherry	50 mL
3 cups	shredded old Cheddar	750 mL
1/2 cup	sliced black olives	125 mL
Dash	hot pepper sauce	Dash
	Salt and freshly ground black pepper	

TOPPING

1 cup	fresh bread crumbs	250 mL
1/2 cup	toasted almonds	125 mL
2 tbsp	grated Parmesan cheese	25 mL

1. Oven Poached Chicken: Place chicken in roasting pan on rack. In a large glass measuring cup, combine chicken stock, wine, bay leaf, tarragon and thyme; pour over

chicken. Cover pan tightly with foil. Bake for 2 hours or until meat thermometer inserted in thickest part of thigh reads 185° F (85° C). Cool chicken in broth.

2. Remove cooled chicken from broth, reserving broth. Remove all meat from carcass, keeping chicken in large strips. Discard skin and bones. Set chicken meat and stock aside separately.

3. Tetrazzini: In a pot of boiling, salted water, cook noodles until tender but still firm, about 5 to 8 minutes. Drain. Rinse under cold running water. Drain and set aside.

4. In a large saucepan, melt 2 tbsp (25 mL) of the butter over medium heat; cook onions, garlic, celery and green pepper for 5 minutes or until softened. Transfer to a large bowl. In same saucepan, melt 2 tbsp (25 mL) of the butter over medium heat; cook mushrooms for 5 minutes or until tender. Add to other vegetables in bowl.

5. Melt remaining butter in same saucepan over medium high heat. Add flour; cook, stirring, until flour pulls away from pan. Remove from heat. Gradually whisk in reserved chicken stock. Return to heat. Cook, stirring until sauce is smooth and thickened. Remove from heat. Whisk in cheese, olives, hot pepper sauce and salt and pepper to taste. Stir in noodles, chicken and vegetables. Spoon into prepared baking dish.

6. Topping: In small bowl, stir together bread crumbs, almonds and Parmesan. Sprinkle evenly over casserole.

To freeze: Wrap well with plastic wrap, then heavy foil. Seal, label and date. Freeze for up to 3 months.

To serve: Thaw in microwave or in refrigerator overnight. Preheat oven to 350° F (180° C). Unwrap casserole. Cover with foil. Bake in center of oven for 20 minutes, uncover and bake another 25 minutes or until heated through.

Quick Chicken and Mushroom Pot Pies

SERVES 4

One of my favorite uses for chicken left from Sunday's roast is a pot pie, and I couldn't resist including one here, even though it meant cheating and baking the pastry separately.

SHOPPING TIP

Brown mushrooms, often the same price as white, are more flavorful.

From Rose Murray: *Quick Chicken*

CRUST (REQUIRED FOR SERVING BUT NOT FREEZING)		
Half	pkg (14 oz [411 g]) puff pastry, thawed	Half
FILLING		
1	egg, beaten	1
2 tbsp	butter	25 mL
8 oz	small mushrooms	250 g
2	carrots, peeled and sliced	2
1	stalk celery, sliced	1
1	onion, chopped	1
1/4 tsp	dried thyme	1 mL
1/4 tsp	dried rosemary	1 mL
1 1/2 cups	chicken stock	375 mL
2 tbsp	cornstarch	25 mL
3 cups	cooked chicken, cut into small pieces	750 mL
1 cup	frozen peas	250 mL
2 tbsp	chopped fresh parsley	25 mL
	Salt and pepper	

1. *If freezing pot pies, proceed to Step 2.* Preheat oven to 400° F (200° C). Roll out enough puff pastry to cut 4 circles slightly bigger than the tops of 4 deep soup bowls. Cut out the circles and place on a cookie sheet; brush with egg and bake in preheated oven for 15 to 20 minutes or until puffed and golden brown.

2. Filling: Meanwhile, in a large saucepan, melt butter over medium heat. Add mushrooms, carrots, celery and onion; cook for 5 minutes. Stir in thyme, rosemary and 1 cup (250 mL) of the stock; bring to a boil. Dissolve the cornstarch in remaining stock and stir into vegetable mixture; cook, stirring, until thickened.

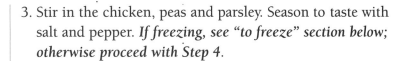

3. Stir in the chicken, peas and parsley. Season to taste with salt and pepper. *If freezing, see "to freeze" section below; otherwise proceed with Step 4.*

4. Transfer to warm soup bowls and top each with a hot pastry round to serve.

To freeze: Let filling cool. Spoon into freezer containers; seal, date and label. Freeze for up to 2 months.

To serve: Thaw filling in microwave or in refrigerator overnight. Proceed with Step 1 to make crust. Heat filling in saucepan until warmed through. Proceed with Step 4, above.

Turkey Pot Pie with Biscuit Topping

SERVES 6

3 tbsp	butter	45 mL
2 cups	sliced mushrooms	500 mL
1/4 cup	flour	50 mL
1 cup	chicken stock	250 mL
2 cups	milk	500 mL
2 tbsp	sherry (optional)	25 mL
1/2 tsp	ground thyme	2 mL
1/2 tsp	ground sage	2 mL
1/2 tsp	salt	2 mL
3 cups	cubed cooked turkey breast	750 mL
4 cups	frozen mixed vegetables	1 L
	Freshly ground black pepper	

There's nothing better than a pot pie when you need to use up leftover turkey or chicken. If you don't have leftovers, purchase a cooked chicken at your grocery store or roast your own turkey breast. Roast one large bone-in turkey breast (2 lbs [1 kg]) at 350° F (180° C) for 70 to 80 minutes or until juices run clear and thermometer registers 170° F (77° C); immediately transfer to the refrigerator and keep for up to 3 days.

AFTER FREEZING/BEFORE SERVING: BISCUIT TOPPING

1 1/2 cups	biscuit baking mix	375 mL
1 tsp	dried parsley	5 mL
7 tbsp	milk	105 mL

From Dietitians of Canada: *Great Food Fast*

1. In a large saucepan, melt 1 tbsp (15 mL) of the butter over medium heat. Add mushrooms and cook for 4 to 5 minutes or until moisture has evaporated, but do not brown. Add remaining butter to pan; stir in flour and blend well. Whisk in stock, milk and, if using, sherry. Stir in thyme, sage and salt; bring to a boil. Reduce heat to low and cook, stirring constantly, for 3 to 5 minutes or until thickened. Remove from heat.

2. Stir in turkey and frozen vegetables. Season to taste with pepper. Spoon into prepared baking dish. *If freezing, see "to freeze" section, below; otherwise proceed with Step 3.*

3. Biscuit Topping: In a bowl combine biscuit mix with parsley; stir in 6 tbsp (75 mL) milk. Gather dough into a ball, adding more baking mix as required to make dough easy to handle. On a lightly floured surface roll out dough to fit top of baking dish; place over filling. Cut a small vent hole in center of topping. Brush with remaining 1 tbsp (15 mL) milk.

4. Bake in center of preheated oven for 35 to 40 minutes or until topping is golden and casserole is bubbling hot.

To freeze: Let casserole cool. Wrap well with plastic wrap, then heavy foil. Seal, label and date. Freeze for up to 3 months.

To serve: Thaw in microwave or in refrigerator overnight. Preheat oven to 350° F (180° C). Unwrap casserole. Proceed with Step 3, above.

Chicken Chili Macaroni

SERVES 4

This quick pasta dish, cooked all in one pan, will be a real family pleaser.

VARIATION

For an Italian version, substitute 1 tsp (5 mL) Italian herb seasoning for the chili powder, use Italian-style stewed tomatoes and 1/2 cup (125 mL) Parmesan cheese for the Monterey Jack cheese. Serve with crusty rolls.

From Rose Murray: *Quick Chicken*

1 lb	lean ground chicken	500 g
1	clove garlic, minced	1
1	can (14 oz [398 mL]) stewed tomatoes, preferably Mexican-style	1
1	can (14 oz [398 mL]) tomato sauce	1
1 tbsp	chili powder	15 mL
1/2 tsp	dried oregano	2 mL
1/2 tsp	ground cumin	2 mL
1 cup	elbow or wagon wheel macaroni	250 mL
1 cup	fresh or frozen cut green beans	250 mL
	Salt and pepper	

AFTER FREEZING/BEFORE SERVING

1 cup	shredded Monterey Jack or Cheddar cheese	250 mL

1. In a large skillet, cook chicken with garlic over medium-high heat, breaking it up with a wooden spoon, for 5 minutes or until chicken is no longer pink.

2. Stir in tomatoes, tomato sauce, chili powder, oregano and cumin. Bring to a boil. Stir in macaroni and green beans; bring back to a boil. Reduce heat to medium-low, cover and cook, stirring occasionally, for 15 minutes or until the pasta and beans are tender. Season to taste with salt and pepper. *If freezing, see "to freeze" section below; otherwise proceed with Step 3.*

3. Serve sprinkled with cheese.

To freeze: Let pasta mixture cool. Spoon into freezer containers; seal, date and label. Freeze for up to 3 months.

To serve: Thaw in microwave or in refrigerator overnight. Reheat in baking dish at 350° F (180° C) for 30 to 35 minutes or until hot and bubbly. Proceed with Step 3, above.

Poppy Seed Noodle Casserole

SERVES 6 TO 8

This can serve as a main dish (with the salmon) or as an accompaniment to meat dishes (without salmon).

TIP

Undercook the pasta if freezing until firm; it will cook further upon reheating. If making to serve immediately, cook pasta a little further. Casseroles that will be frozen should always have extra liquid because they absorb moisture as they reheat.

Frozen herbs have all the taste and texture of just picked. Whenever you can, pick, wash, chop and freeze herbs. It saves so much time to have them ready to add to a recipe.

8-CUP (2 L) CASSEROLE, GREASED

1		pkg (12 oz [375 g]) egg noodles	1
2 tbsp		vegetable oil	25 mL
1 cup		chopped onions	250 mL
2		cloves garlic, minced	2
2 cups		1% cottage cheese	500 mL
1 cup		sour cream	250 mL
1/4 cup		poppy seeds	50 mL
1 tbsp		chopped fresh tarragon or dill	15 mL
1		can (6 oz [113 g]) salmon, drained (optional)	1
1 tbsp		grated Parmesan cheese (optional)	15 mL

1. In pot of boiling, salted water, cook noodles until tender but still firm, about 8 minutes. Drain. Rinse under cold running water. Drain and set aside.

2. In a saucepan, heat oil over medium-high heat. Add onions and garlic; cook for 5 minutes or until softened.

3. In food processor, combine cottage cheese and sour cream; purée until smooth. Add onion mixture, poppy seeds, tarragon and salmon (if using). Pulse on and off until well combined. Transfer to a large bowl; stir in noodles. Pour into prepared dish. Sprinkle with Parmesan, if using. *If freezing, see "to freeze" section below; otherwise proceed with Step 4.*

4. Preheat oven to 350° F (180° C). Cover and bake in center of oven for 40 to 45 minutes or until heated through.

To freeze: Wrap well with plastic wrap, then foil; seal, date and label. Freeze for up to 3 months.

To serve: Thaw in microwave or in refrigerator overnight. Unwrap baking dish and proceed with Step 4, above.

Chicken and Broccoli Pasta with Pesto

SERVES 4

This colorful main dish takes only minutes to make.

SHOPPING TIP

To save time, buy pre-cut broccoli florets and chicken already cut in strips.

SERVING SUGGESTIONS

Spinach and Mushroom Salad: For a homemade dressing to top fresh spinach and sliced mush-rooms, whisk together 1/3 cup (75 mL) light sour cream, 2 tbsp (25 mL) each milk and light mayon-naise, 2 tsp (10 mL) each granulated sugar and cider vinegar, a minced garlic clove, and salt and pepper to taste.

Cinnamon Bananas with Honey Yogurt: Cut peeled bananas lengthwise, sprinkle with brown sugar, dots of butter and cinnamon; broil close to the element for 3 to 5 minutes and serve with plain yogurt sweetened with honey.

From Rose Murray: *Quick Chicken*

12 oz	penne	375 g
2 tbsp	olive oil	25 mL
1 lb	boneless, skinless chicken breasts cut into 1/2-inch (1 cm) strips	500 g
1	red bell pepper, cut into strips	1
8 oz	small broccoli florets (4 cups [1 L])	250 g
1	container (6.5 oz [185 g]) pesto (about 3/4 cup [175 mL])	1
1/3 cup	freshly grated Parmesan cheese	75 mL

AFTER FREEZING/BEFORE SERVING

	Additional freshly grated Parmesan	

1. In a large pot of boiling salted water, cook the penne for 8 to 10 minutes or until tender but firm.

2. Meanwhile, in a large skillet, heat oil over medium-high heat. Add chicken and red pepper; cook for 3 to 5 minutes, stirring often, or until the chicken is cooked through. Set aside.

3. Place the broccoli in a colander and drain the pasta over it. Place back in the pot. Stir in the pesto, the contents of the skillet and the cheese. *If freezing, see "to freeze" section below; otherwise proceed with Step 4.*

4. Serve immediately with additional cheese for sprinkling at the table.

To freeze: Let mixture cool. Spoon into freezer containers, allowing headspace; seal, date and label. Freeze for up to 3 months.

To serve: Thaw in microwave or in refrigerator overnight. Bake in baking dish at 350° F (180° C) for 30 to 35 minutes or until heated through. Proceed with Step 4, above.

Veal Stew with Dill and Mushrooms

SERVES 6

The combination of veal with dill and mushrooms is a tantalizing blend. It works well with pork too. Serve either one with a barley or noodle casserole (see recipe, page 105) and salad for a complete meal.

TIP

You can freeze the stew completely made, but freezing it after Step 2 and then stirring in sour cream-flour mixture when reheating thawed stew gives a fresher flavor.

VARIATION

Pork with Dill and Mushrooms: Substitute pork butt for the veal.

2 tbsp	vegetable oil	25 mL
3 lbs	stewing veal or pork, cut in cubes	1.5 kg
2 cups	chopped onions	500 mL
2	cloves garlic, minced	2
2 cups	Basic Chicken Stock (see recipe, page 69)	500 mL
1 cup	dry white wine	250 mL
1 lb	mushrooms, sliced	500 g
1	carrot, diced	1
1/4 cup	finely chopped fresh dill	50 mL
1/4 cup	finely chopped fresh parsley	50 mL
1/2 tsp	dried thyme leaves	2 mL
1	bay leaf	1
	Salt and freshly ground black pepper	

AFTER FREEZING/BEFORE SERVING

1 cup	sour cream	250 mL
2 tbsp	all-purpose flour	25 mL

1. In a large saucepan, heat oil over medium-high heat. In batches, brown pork, transferring to bowl as browned.

2. Return all pork to saucepan. Stir in onions and garlic; cover and cook for 5 minutes or until onions are softened. Stir in chicken stock, wine, mushrooms, carrot, dill, parsley, thyme and bay leaf. Bring to a boil. Reduce heat; simmer, covered, for 40 minutes or until meat is tender. Season with salt and pepper. Remove bay leaf. *If freezing, see "to freeze" section below; otherwise proceed with Step 3.*

3. In a small bowl, stir together sour cream and flour; stir into stew. Cook over medium heat, stirring constantly, until gravy thickens.

To freeze: Let mixture cool. Spoon into freezer containers; seal, date and label. Freeze for up to 2 months.

To serve: Thaw in microwave or in refrigerator overnight. Reheat. Proceed with Step 3, above.

Pork Apple Curry

SERVES 6 TO 8

An every day sweet curry is given a party touch when served with bowls of cashews, yogurt, chutney and toasted coconut as condiments.

TIP

Remember that the spices may change a little on freezing. Taste, and adjust seasoning after freezing.

VARIATION

Chicken Apple Curry: Substitute 2 lb (1 kg) boneless, skinless chicken thighs for pork or lamb.

1/4 cup	vegetable oil	50 mL
2 cups	chopped onion	500 mL
2 tbsp	grated ginger root	25 mL
1 tbsp	curry powder	15 mL
2	cloves garlic, minced	2
Pinch	cayenne pepper	Pinch
2 lbs	pork butt or boneless lamb, cut into 1-inch (2 cm) pieces	1 kg
3 to 4 cups	tomato juice	750 mL to 1 L
2 cups	sliced peeled apples	500 mL
1 cup	raisins	250 mL

1. In a large saucepan, heat oil over medium heat. Add onions, ginger, curry, garlic and cayenne; cook for 10 minutes or until onions are softened. Stir in pork or lamb; cook for 10 to 15 minutes or until browned.

2. Stir in 3 cups (750 mL) tomato juice. Bring to a boil. Reduce heat; simmer covered for 30 minutes. Stir in apples and raisins; simmer another 20 minutes or until meat is tender. Add extra tomato juice if sauce becomes too thick.

To freeze: Let mixture cool. Spoon into freezer containers; seal, date and label. Freeze for up to 2 months.

To serve: Thaw in microwave or in refrigerator overnight. Reheat.

Goulash

Pork or veal can be used in this Hungarian stew. Serve with Much More Mash (see recipe, page 116).

TIP

You can freeze the stew completely made, but freezing it after Step 3 and then stirring in sour cream-flour mixture when reheating thawed stew gives a fresher flavor.

If you prefer, beef stock may be substituted for wine in this stew.

2 lbs	trimmed pork shoulder, butt chops or stewing veal, cut into 1-inch (2 cm) cubes	1 kg
2 tbsp	all-purpose flour	25 mL
2 tbsp	vegetable oil	25 mL
1 1/2 cups	chopped onions	375 mL
2	cloves garlic, minced	2
2 tbsp	Hungarian paprika	25 mL
1	can (28 oz [796 L]) sauerkraut, drained and rinsed	1
1 1/2 cups	Basic Chicken Stock (see recipe, page 69)	375 mL
1 cup	dry white wine	250 mL
1/4 cup	tomato paste	50 mL
1 tbsp	caraway seeds	15 mL
1	bay leaf	1
	Salt and freshly ground black pepper	

AFTER FREEZING/BEFORE SERVING

1 1/2 cups	sour cream 375 mL	
2 tbsp	all-purpose flour	25 mL

1. In a bowl toss pork with flour.

2. In a large saucepan, heat oil over medium-high heat. In batches, cook meat until browned on all sides. Return all meat to saucepan. Stir in onions and garlic; cover and cook over medium heat for 5 minutes or until onions are softened.

3. Stir in paprika, sauerkraut, stock, wine, tomato paste, caraway seeds and bay leaf. Bring to a boil. Reduce heat; simmer, covered, for 40 to 45 minutes or until tender. Season to taste with salt and pepper. Discard bay leaf. *If freezing, see "to freeze" section below; otherwise proceed with Step 4.*

4. In a small bowl, stir together sour cream and flour; stir into stew. Cook over medium heat, stirring constantly, until gravy thickens. Serve with mashed potatoes.

To freeze: Let mixture cool. Spoon into freezer containers; seal, date and label. Freeze for up to 2 months.

To serve: Thaw in microwave or in refrigerator overnight. Reheat. Proceed with Step 4, above.

Beef Bourgignon

SERVES 6

This is a classic stew from the Burgundy area of France. It doubles as a week night meal and a wonderful buffet dish to serve for a party. To serve for the weeknight, divide it into usable portions before freezing.

TIP

If not freezing, but making to serve immediately, add 2 cups (500 mL) of potato balls at step 4 with the pearl onions.

2	slices bacon, chopped	2
1/4 cup	all-purpose flour	50 mL
1/2 tsp	salt	2 mL
1/4 tsp	freshly ground black pepper	1 mL
2 lbs	stewing beef, cut into 1-inch (2 cm) cubes	1 kg
	Vegetable oil	
2	onions, chopped	2
2	cloves garlic, minced	2
1	carrot, chopped	1
1 cup	beef stock	250 mL
1 cup	red wine	250 mL
1	bay leaf	1
1 tsp	dried thyme leaves	5 mL
8 oz	button mushrooms	250 g
2 tbsp	butter (optional)	25 mL
1 tsp	granulated sugar (optional)	5 mL
2 cups	pearl onions (optional)	500 mL
AFTER FREEZING/BEFORE SERVING		
1/4 cup	chopped fresh parsley	50 mL

1. In a large saucepan or Dutch oven, cook bacon over medium heat until browned and fat has rendered. Meanwhile, In a bowl stir together flour, salt and pepper. Toss meat in flour mixture; add to saucepan. Cook in batches until browned on all sides adding a little oil as needed. Stir in onions and garlic; cover and cook for 10 minutes or until onions are softened.

2. Add carrot, beef stock, wine, bay leaf, thyme and mushrooms. Bring to a boil. Reduce heat; simmer, covered, for 1 1/2 to 2 hours or until meat is tender.

3. Meanwhile, if using onions, melt butter over medium heat; stir in sugar and pearl onions. Cook until browned. Stir pearl onions into stew; simmer stew another 20 minutes or until vegetables are tender. *If freezing, see "to freeze" section below; otherwise proceed with Step 4.*

4. Serve sprinkled with fresh parsley.

To freeze: Let mixture cool. Spoon into freezer containers; seal, date and label. Freeze for up to 1 month.

To serve: Thaw in microwave or in refrigerator overnight. Reheat. Proceed with Step 4, above.

Carbonnade

This hearty beef stew, of Flemish ancestry, owes its smooth, rich flavor to a slow braise in dark beer. It freezes well and doubles easily for a crowd. Like all good stews, this carbonnade tastes better the second day.

VARIATION

Carbonnade Casserole: Instead of reheating the stew stove top, spoon into a casserole dish and place croutons on top. Cover. Bake in 350° F (180° C) oven for 45 minutes or until heated through.

1/4 cup	all-purpose flour	50 mL
1/2 tsp	salt	2 mL
1/4 tsp	freshly ground black pepper	1 mL
2 lbs	stewing beef	1 kg
2 tbsp	vegetable oil	25 mL
2	large onions, sliced	2
2	cloves garlic, minced	2
1	bottle (10 oz [341 mL]) beer	1
1 1/2 cups	beef stock	375 mL
2 tbsp	packed brown sugar	25 mL
2 tbsp	wine vinegar	25 mL
2	bay leaves	2
1 tsp	dried thyme leaves	5 mL
1/2 tsp	salt	2 mL
1/4 tsp	freshly ground nutmeg	1 mL
1/4 tsp	freshly ground black pepper	1 mL
AFTER FREEZING/BEFORE SERVING: MUSTARD CROUTONS		
3	slices French bread, crusts removed	3
2 tbsp	Dijon mustard	45 mL

1. In a bowl stir together flour, 1/2 tsp (2 mL) salt and 1/4 tsp (1 mL) pepper. Toss meat in flour mixture.

2. In a large saucepan or Dutch oven, heat oil over medium-high heat. In batches, cook meat until browned on all sides. Return all beef to saucepan. Stir in onions and garlic; cover and cook 5 minutes or until onions are softened. Add beer, beef stock, brown sugar, vinegar, bay leaves, thyme, 1/2 tsp (2 mL) salt, nutmeg and 1/4 tsp (1 mL) pepper. Bring to a boil. Reduce heat; simmer, covered, for 1 1/2 to 2 hours, stirring occasionally, or until meat is tender. Discard bay leaves. *If freezing, see "to freeze" section below; otherwise proceed with Step 3.*

4. Preheat oven to 350° F (180° C). Spread bread with mustard and place on baking sheet. Bake for 15 minutes or until toasted. Cut into 1/2-inch (1 cm) cubes. Serve stew sprinkled with croutons.

To freeze: Let mixture cool. Spoon into freezer containers; seal, date and label. Freeze for up to 2 months.

To serve: Thaw in microwave or in refrigerator overnight. Reheat. Proceed with Step 4.

Coq Au Vin

SERVES 6

This French provincial dish typically uses red wine; however, I prefer the more mellow flavor of dry sherry to braise the chicken. You need chicken parts that lend themselves to simmering — leg pieces, not breasts.

TIP

To save time, substitute 2 1/2 lbs (1.25 kg) boneless skinless chicken thighs; reduce cooking time to about 30 minutes.

3 lbs	chicken legs, thighs or drumsticks	1.5 kg
1 tbsp	vegetable oil	15 mL
6	slices bacon, chopped	6
2 cups	chopped onions	500 mL
1 cup	chopped carrots	250 mL
2	cloves garlic, minced	2
8 oz	mushrooms, quartered	250 g
3 tbsp	all-purpose flour	45 mL
1 1/2 cups	Basic Chicken Stock (see recipe, page 69)	375 mL
1 cup	dry sherry or red wine	250 mL
1/2 tsp	dried marjoram	2 mL
1/2 tsp	dried thyme leaves	2 mL
1	bay leaf	1
2 cups	pearl onions (optional)	500 mL
AFTER FREEZING/BEFORE SERVING		
1/2 cup	chopped fresh parsley	125 mL
1 tsp	salt	5 mL
1/4 tsp	freshly ground black pepper	1 mL

1. Remove skin from chicken pieces. If using legs, divide into thighs and drumsticks.

2. In a large saucepan over medium-high heat, cook oil, bacon, onions, carrots and garlic for 5 minutes or until onion is softened and bacon browned. With slotted spoon, remove vegetables to bowl, leaving behind as much bacon and fat as possible. Add chicken to pan in batches, turning to brown well on all sides.

3. Stir in mushrooms; cook until liquid is released. Stir in onion mixture. Sprinkle with flour; cook, stirring, until it forms a paste. Gradually whisk in stock and sherry and stock. Cook for 3 to 4 minutes or until thickened. Stir in marjoram, thyme, bay leaf and pearl onions, if using. Bring to a boil. Reduce heat; simmer, covered, for 45 minutes, stirring occasionally, or until chicken is tender and falling off the bone. Discard bay leaf. *If freezing, see "to freeze" section below; otherwise proceed with Step 4.*

4. Stir in parsley, salt and pepper before serving.

To freeze: Let mixture cool. Spoon into freezer containers; seal, date and label. Freeze for up to 2 months.

To serve: Thaw in microwave or in refrigerator overnight. Reheat. Proceed with Step 4, above.

Much more mash

For all those potato purists, here's the real McCoy, along with some tempting variations that are well worth trying.

KITCHEN WISDOM

About 8 medium potatoes equals 2 1/2 lbs (1.25 kg).

MAKE AHEAD

Mashed potatoes can be refrigerated, covered, for up to 3 days. Reheat, covered, in the microwave on High for 6 to 8 minutes, or in a 350° F (180° C) oven for 30 minutes until piping hot.

2 1/2 lbs	baking potatoes, such as Yukon Gold, peeled and cut into 2-inch (5 cm) chunks	1.25 kg
1/4 tsp	salt	1 mL
1/2 cup	milk	125 mL
2 tbsp	butter or olive oil	25 mL
1/4 tsp	black pepper	1 mL
	Chopped fresh parsley	

1. In a large saucepan over high heat, combine potatoes and just enough cold water to cover them. Add salt; bring to a boil. Reduce heat to medium-low; cook, covered, for 20 to 25 minutes or until potatoes are very tender. Drain well; return potatoes to saucepan. Place over low heat to dry out potatoes slightly, shaking saucepan occasionally to prevent them from sticking.

2. Meanwhile, in a small microwaveable bowl, heat milk and butter or oil in microwave on High for 1 to 2 minutes or until steaming. (Alternatively, heat milk and butter or oil in a saucepan over medium-high heat until steaming.) Add milk mixture to potatoes; mash roughly with a fork. With an electric mixer, beat potatoes until smooth and creamy. (Don't overbeat or potatoes will become gluey.) Add pepper. If desired, season to taste with additional salt and pepper. Spoon into a warm serving dish. Sprinkle with parsley; serve at once.

VARIATIONS

Pesto Potatoes

Omit butter or oil; add 1/4 cup (50 mL) each pesto and freshly grated Parmesan cheese before beating.

Mustard Mash

Use butter instead of oil; add 1/4 cup (50 mL) grainy Dijon mustard before beating.

Lemony Mash

Use oil instead of butter; add 1/4 cup (50 mL) chopped fresh parsley and 1 tbsp (15 mL) finely grated lemon zest before beating.

Cheese and Onion Mash

Use butter instead of oil; add 1 cup (250 mL) shredded Cheddar or Swiss cheese and 1/4 cup (50 mL) finely chopped green onions before beating.

Posh French Mash

This is called *aligot* in France and is positively délicieux. Add 2 peeled cloves of garlic to potatoes before boiling. Drain well, retaining garlic with potatoes. Mash as above, using butter instead of oil and adding 1 cup (250 mL) shredded Gruyère cheese before beating.

Caesar Potatoes

Omit butter or oil; add 1/2 cup (125 mL) thick Caesar dressing and 1/4 cup (50 mL) freshly grated Parmesan cheese before beating.

Bavarian Stew

SERVES 4 TO 6

A hearty stew with sweet and sour flavors. It is best served over noodles, (see recipe, page 105) and accompanied by red cabbage.

TIP

The red cabbage can be made ahead and frozen as a separate casserole. It keeps well for up to 2 months. Thaw in the microwave or in the refrigerator and reheat.

2 lbs	stewing beef, cut into 1 1/2-inch (4 cm) cubes	1 kg
2 tbsp	vegetable oil	25 mL
2 cups	chopped onions	500 mL
1	clove garlic, minced	1
2 tbsp	all-purpose flour	25 mL
3 cups	beef stock	750 mL
1/2 cup	red wine vinegar	125 mL
1/4 cup	molasses	50 mL
2 tbsp	packed brown sugar	25 mL
2 tsp	caraway seeds	10 mL
1 tsp	ground cinnamon	5 mL
1/2 tsp	ground ginger	2 mL
1/4 tsp	ground cloves	1 mL
1	bay leaf	1
	Salt and freshly ground black pepper	

AFTER FREEZING/BEFORE SERVING: RED CABBAGE

2 tbsp	butter	25 mL
6 cups	shredded red cabbage	1.5 L
2	apples, peeled, cored and sliced	2
1/2 cup	chopped onion	125 mL
1 cup	hot water	250 mL
1/4 cup	packed brown sugar	50 mL
2 tbsp	red wine vinegar	25 mL
1	bay leaf	1

1. In a large saucepan, heat oil over medium-high heat. Add beef in batches and cook until browned.

2. Return all beef to saucepan. Stir in onions and garlic; cover and cook over medium heat for 5 minutes or until onions are softened. Sprinkle flour over meat; cook, stirring, until flour draws away from pan. Pour in stock. Cook, stirring, for 5 minutes or until smooth and thickened.

3. Stir in vinegar, molasses, brown sugar, caraway seeds, cinnamon, ginger, cloves and bay leaf. Bring to a boil. Reduce heat; simmer, covered, for 1 1/2 to 2 hours or until meat is tender. Season to taste with salt and pepper. Discard bay leaf. *If freezing, see "to freeze" section below; otherwise proceed with Steps 4 and 5.*

4. Red Cabbage: In a saucepan melt butter over medium heat. Stir in cabbage, apples and onions; cover and cook 5 to 10 minutes or until softened. Stir in water, brown sugar, vinegar and bay leaf. Cook uncovered for 15 to 20 minutes or until vegetables are very tender and most of liquid has evaporated.

5. Serve stew over noodles, topped with red cabbage.

To freeze: Let mixture cool. Spoon into freezer containers; seal, date and label. Freeze for up to 2 months.

To serve: Thaw in microwave or in refrigerator overnight. Reheat stew. Meanwhile, proceed with Steps 4 and 5, above.

Basic Tomato Sauce

MAKES ABOUT 4 CUPS (1 L)

Excellent on pasta or pizza. It ca also be adapted for soups and fillings. Feel free to change the herbs to your favorites. Tarragon and parsley could be added if oregano is omitted.

1/4 cup	vegetable oil	50 mL
1 cup	chopped onions	250 mL
3	cloves garlic, minced	3
1	can (28 oz [796 mL]) diced tomatoes	1
1	can (5 1/2 oz [142 mL]) tomato paste	1
1/4 cup	red wine	50 mL
1 tbsp	granulated sugar	15 mL
1 tsp	dried basil	5 mL
1/2 tsp	dried oregano	2 mL
1/4 tsp	dried thyme leaves	1 mL
	Salt and freshly ground black pepper	

1. In a saucepan heat oil over medium-high heat. Stir in onions and garlic; cover and cook for 5 minutes or until onions are soft.

2. Stir in tomatoes, tomato paste, wine, sugar, basil, oregano and thyme. Bring to a boil, crushing tomatoes as you stir. Reduce heat; simmer, uncovered, for 30 minutes. Season to taste with salt and pepper.

To freeze: Let mixture cool. Spoon into freezer containers; seal, date and label. Freeze for up to 3 months.

To serve: Thaw in microwave or in refrigerator overnight. Reheat if desired.

Winter Pesto Sauce

PREHEAT OVEN TO 350 F (180 C)

MAKES
1 1/3 CUPS
(325 mL)

Because you don't need fresh basil for this sauce, you can make it year-round. Its addictive flavor is excellent on pasta, as a salad dressing with added vinegar, as a sauce for fish or on croustades (see recipe, page 128).

VARIATION

Sun-Dried Tomato Pesto: Add 1/2 cup (125 mL) diced oil-packed sun-dried tomatoes at Step 2.

1/4 cup	pine nuts	50 mL
2 cups	packed fresh parsley leaves	500 mL
1/2 cup	grated Parmesan cheese	125 mL
2 tbsp	dried basil	25 mL
3	cloves garlic, chopped	3
1/2 tsp	salt	2 mL
1/4 tsp	freshly ground black pepper	1 mL
3/4 cup	extra virgin olive oil	175 mL

1. Spread pine nuts on baking sheet. Toast for 10 minutes or until golden and fragrant. Cool.

2. In food processor, combine pine nuts, parsley, cheese, basil, garlic, salt and pepper. Process until finely chopped. With motor running, add oil through the feed tube.

To freeze: Spoon into freezer containers; seal, date and label. Freeze for up to 4 months.

To serve: Thaw in microwave or in refrigerator overnight.

Leek and Seafood Sauce

**MAKES 5 CUPS
(1.25 L)**

This can be made with fresh or frozen seafood. To prevent toughening seafood, add fish when you reheat the thawed sauce. Serve over rice or pasta with crusty bread.

2 tbsp	butter	25 mL
2 cups	sliced leeks	500 mL
1	clove garlic, minced	1
2 tsp	all-purpose flour	25 mL
1	can (28 oz [796 mL]) tomatoes, finely chopped	1
1/2 cup	dry white wine	125 mL
1 tbsp	dried tarragon	15 mL
1 tsp	granulated sugar	5 mL
1/2 tsp	ground fennel	2 mL
1/2 tsp	dried thyme leaves	2 mL
1	bay leaf	1
1	2-inch (5 cm) piece orange zest	1
Dash	hot pepper sauce	Dash
AFTER FREEZING/BEFORE SERVING		
1 lb	scallops, shelled shrimp or cod, cut into 1-inch (2.5 cm) cubes	500 g

1. In a heavy saucepan, melt butter over medium heat. Add leeks and garlic; cook 5 to 7 minutes or until softened.

2. Sprinkle with flour. Cook, stirring, until mixture pulls away from pan. Stir in tomatoes and juices; cook how long, stirring, or until thickened. Stir in wine, tarragon, sugar, fennel, thyme, bay leaf, orange zest and pepper sauce. Bring to a boil; reduce heat and simmer for 20 minutes. Discard bay leaf and orange zest. *If freezing, see "to freeze" section below; otherwise proceed with Step 3.*

3. Bring sauce to a boil. Stir in seafood or fish; reduce heat to simmer and cook for 5 minutes or until fish is opaque.

To freeze: Spoon into freezer containers; seal, date and label. Freeze for up to 3 months.

To serve: Thaw in microwave or in refrigerator overnight. Proceed with Step 3, above.

Sausage and Tomato Sauce

MAKES 6 CUPS (1.5 L)

A mellow spaghetti sauce full of sliced Italian sausage. Serve with freshly grated Parmesan over fettuccine or spaghettini.

2 tbsp	olive oil	25 mL
1 cup	chopped onion	250 mL
1	green pepper, chopped	1
3	cloves garlic, minced	3
1	can (28 oz [796 mL]) tomatoes	1
1	can (5 1/2 oz [156 mL]) tomato paste	1
1/2 cup	dry white wine	125 mL
2 tsp	granulated sugar	10 mL
2 tsp	dried basil	10 mL
1/2 tsp	dried thyme leaves	2 mL
1	bay leaf	1
1 lb	Italian sausage	500 g
	Salt and freshly ground black pepper	

1. In a large saucepan, heat oil over medium heat. Add onion, green pepper and garlic; cook, covered, for 5 to 7 minutes or until softened. Stir into tomatoes and juices, tomato paste, wine, sugar, basil, thyme and bay leaf. Bring to a boil. Reduce heat; simmer, covered, for 45 minutes.

2. Meanwhile, in a saucepan, arrange sausage in a single layer. Pour in about 1/2 inch (1 cm) water and bring to a boil. Reduce heat to simmer; cook for about 10 minutes or until sausage are no longer pink inside. Drain and cool. Cut sausages into 1-inch (2.5 cm) slices.

3. Stir sausages into sauce. Season to taste with salt and pepper.

To freeze: Spoon into freezer containers; seal, date and label. Freeze for up to 4 months.

To serve: Thaw in microwave or in refrigerator overnight. Reheat.

Mushroom Cream Sauce

**MAKES ABOUT
3 CUPS (750 mL)
SERVES 4**

A wickedly rich sauce, ideal
for easy entertaining.

2 tbsp	butter	25 mL
12 oz	mushrooms (preferably brown), sliced	375 g
1	clove garlic, minced	1
1/2 tsp	freshly grated nutmeg	2 mL
1/2 tsp	dried thyme leaves	2 mL
1/2 cup	dry white wine	125 mL
1/2 cup	chicken stock	125 mL
2 cups	whipping (35%) cream	500 mL
1/3 cup	finely chopped fresh parsley	75 mL
	Salt and freshly ground black pepper	

1. In large frying pan, melt butter over medium-high heat. Add mushrooms, garlic, nutmeg and thyme; cook for about 5 to 8 minutes or until mushrooms are tender.

2. Stir in wine and stock; cook until liquid is reduced by half. Stir in whipping cream. Bring to a boil. Reduce heat; simmer, uncovered, for 5 minutes or until sauce has thickened enough to coat the back of a spoon. Stir in parsley. Season to taste with salt and pepper.

To freeze: Spoon into freezer containers; seal, date and label. Freeze for up to 2 months.

To serve: Thaw in microwave or in refrigerator overnight. Reheat sauce and toss with cooked fettuccine and a bowl of grated Parmesan cheese.

entertaining

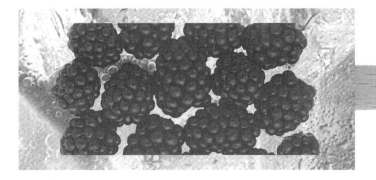

Entertaining ideas

How many times have you spent the whole day preparing food for a dinner party – and then were too tired to entertain your guests? With a freezer, this never need happen again. The freezer allows you to prepare the food in stages, freezing where necessary, so that everything is ready by the day of your special occasion.

Freezing for entertaining is not long-term storage, usually just a period of several weeks. Start with the baking – preparing and freezing cakes, breads, cookies and pastries. Casserole dishes, soups and stews come next. If you're preparing a frozen dessert, this comes last. Of course, fresh salads and dressings are not frozen, but prepared a day or two ahead and refrigerated.

Menu planning

The first thing to do is choose a menu suitable for the event, the season and the tastes of the people who are going to come. Keep in mind that the larger the crowd, the simpler the menu should be.

Once you decide on your menu, write down a practical work plan. Start with the dish that can be made first and estimate a realistic preparation time for both shopping, cooking and clean-up. Make sure you have the necessary freezing dishes. Don't be overly ambitious. Plan a realistic amount of preparation that can be undertaken at one time – especially if you are cooking for a large group. It is better to do one dish a day and not be exhausted.

Remember to include time for thawing frozen food. Baked goods can be thawed on the counter the day of the event. Casseroles, soups and stews can be thawed in the refrigerator a day ahead. To save time with clean-up and serving, try to freeze food in dishes that can also be used for baking and serving.

Herbed Cheese Dip or Spread

MAKES ABOUT 3 CUPS (750 mL)

1	large clove garlic, minced	1
1/2 cup	chopped fresh parsley	125 mL
2	green onions, chopped	2
8 oz	cream cheese, softened	250 g
1/4 cup	sliced pimento-stuffed olives	50 mL
2 tbsp	fresh lemon juice	25 mL
1 tsp	Worcestershire sauce	5 mL
Dash	hot pepper sauce	Dash
1 tsp	finely chopped fresh thyme, tarragon or basil	5 mL
1/2 tsp	salt	2 mL
1/4 tsp	freshly ground black pepper	1 mL
AFTER FREEZING/BEFORE SERVING		
1 cup	sour cream	250 mL

1. In food processor, combine garlic, parsley and green onions. Process until finely chopped and well mixed. Add cream cheese, olives, lemon juice, Worcestershire, hot pepper sauce, thyme, salt and pepper; purée until smooth. *If freezing, see "to freeze" section below; otherwise proceed with Step 2.*

2. Stir in sour cream. Serve with crudités, crackers or sliced baguette.

To freeze: Spoon into freezer containers; seal, label and date. Freeze for up to 2 months.

To serve: Thaw in refrigerator overnight. Proceed with Step 2, above.

Pesto Croustades

MAKES ABOUT 24

These "mini pizzas" are delectable served as a appetizer or as a companion to soup.

1	baguette	1
1 cup	Winter Pesto Sauce (see recipe, page 121) or Basil Pesto (see recipe, page 54)	250 mL
3/4 cup	oil-packed sun-dried tomatoes, drained	175 mL
2 cups	shredded mozzarella cheese	500 mL

1. Slice bread into 3/4-inch (2 cm) pieces. Spread each with about 2 tsp (10 mL) pesto.

2. Cut sun-dried tomatoes into 1-inch (2 cm) pieces. Arrange one in center of each baguette slice. Sprinkle with mozzarella. Place on baking sheets. *If freezing, see "to freeze" section below; otherwise proceed with Step 3.*

3. Preheat oven to 350° F (180° C). Bake croustades for 8 to 10 minutes or until cheese is melted.

To freeze: Wrap well; seal, label and date. Freeze for up to 1 month.

To serve: Bake from frozen. Proceed with Step 3, above, increasing baking time to 12 to 15 minutes.

SIZZLING SHRIMP (PAGE 129) ➤
OVERLEAF: DOUBLE CHOCOLATE CHUNK COOKIES (PAGE 176)

Sizzling Shrimp

SERVES 6

This messy but delectable first course is perfect for sharing among good friends. Serve straight from the baking dish with good-quality crusty bread to mop up the spicy olive oil.

From Julia Aitken: Easy Entertaining

PREHEAT OVEN TO 450° F (230° C)
9-INCH (22.5 CM) OVENPROOF EARTHENWARE DISH OR GLASS PIE PLATE

1 1/2 lbs	raw large shrimp, peeled and deveined, patted dry	750 g
3	cloves garlic, sliced	3
1/4 tsp	salt	1 mL
1/4 tsp	hot pepper flakes	1 mL
1/2 cup	olive oil	125 mL

1. Spread out shrimp in baking dish; tuck slices of garlic in amongst shrimp. Sprinkle with salt and hot pepper flakes. Drizzle oil evenly over shrimp.

2. Preheat oven to 350° F (180° C). Bake for 10 to 12 minutes, stirring once or twice, until shrimp are pink and opaque and oil is bubbling. Serve at once.

FREEZER TIP

You could prepare and freeze this dish, but why bother? It's a snap to make with thawed frozen shrimp which have already been shelled and deveined.

◄ EASY BOUILLABAISSE (PAGE 136)

Mini Cheese Soufflés

MAKES ABOUT 90

No one will guess that
these melt-in-the-mouth
puffs are a breeze to make
straight from your freezer to
the oven.

1	1 1/2-lb (750 g) loaf plain white bread, unsliced	1
4	egg whites	4
8 oz	cream cheese, softened	250 g
2 1/2 cups	shredded old Cheddar cheese	625 mL
1 cup	melted butter	250 mL
1 tsp	Dijon mustard	5 mL

1. Using a bread knife, carefully cut crusts from all sides of loaf of bread. Slice bread into 1-inch (2 cm) slices. Cut each slice into nine cubes. Place in container and store in freezer while proceeding with recipe.

2. In a bowl with an electric mixer, beat egg whites until stiff peaks form.

3. In another bowl using an electric mixer, beat cream cheese, Cheddar, butter and mustard together. Fold in egg whites. Spread over each side of each bread cube, arranging in single layer on baking sheet as each one is spread. *If freezing, see "to freeze" section below; otherwise proceed with Step 3.*

3. Preheat oven to 400° F (200° C). Arrange soufflés on baking sheet lined with parchment paper. Bake for 8 to 10 minutes or until golden brown. Serve immediately.

To freeze: Cover baking sheet and freeze for 1 hour or until frozen. Transfer to freezer bags or containers; seal, label and date. Freeze for up to 1 month.

To serve: Bake from frozen. Proceed with Step 3, above, increasing baking time to 10 minutes.

Choux Pastry for Bouchées

Makes about 48

This recipe is the backbone of many delectable concoctions. As a savory, bouchées can be split and filled with your favorite, seafood, chicken, ham or cheese mixture. As a sweet, they can be filled with sweetened whipped cream and drizzled with chocolate ganache (melted bittersweet chocolate truffle mixture) or simply sprinkled with sifted confectioner's (icing) sugar. Try the examples below.

Variations

Cheese Gougères: Stir 1/2 cup (125 mL) grated Parmesan and 2 tsp (10 mL) chopped fresh thyme into the batter before dropping batter onto baking sheet and freezing. Serve plain rather than filling.

Chocolate Eclairs: Pipe or spoon plain batter onto sheets into long fingers about 3 inch (7.5 cm) long. Fill split baked eclairs with sweetened whipped cream and drizzle with melted Bittersweet Truffle mixture (see page 144).

1 cup	water	250 mL
1/2 cup	butter	125 mL
1 cup	all-purpose flour	250 mL
4	eggs	4
1/4 tsp	salt	1 mL

1. In saucepan combine water and butter. Bring to a boil over medium-high heat. Once butter has melted, remove from heat. Using electric mixer, beat in flour all at once. Continue to beat until mixture leaves sides of saucepan.

2. Beat in eggs, one at a time. Continue to beat until batter is smooth, glossy and mounds when dropped from a spoon. Beat in salt. Drop batter in 1 tbsp (15 mL) amounts onto baking sheets lined with parchment paper, spacing bouchées 2-inches (5 cm) apart. *If freezing, see "to freeze" section below; otherwise proceed with Step 3.*

3. Preheat oven to 375° F (190° C). Bake for 25 to 30 minutes or until puffs are doubled in size and golden. Transfer to wire rack to cool. Slice in half horizontally and fill.

To freeze: Cover baking sheet and freeze for 1 hour or until firm. Cover well with plastic wrap; seal, label and date. Freeze for up to 2 months.

To serve: Bake from frozen. Proceed with Step 3, above, increasing baking time to 25 to 30 minutes.

Savory Cheese Shortbread

LARGE BAKING SHEET LINED WITH PARCHMENT PAPER

MAKES ABOUT 24

1 cup	all-purpose flour	250 mL
1 cup	grated old Cheddar cheese	250 mL
1/2 cup	butter, softened	125 mL
Pinch	cayenne pepper	Pinch

You can never go wrong if you have a batch of these mouth-watering "cookies" in the freezer. They can be kept frozen for up to 6 months and go from freezer to oven. A perfect nibble with a glass of wine!

TIP

To lightly flour ball, dip into your flour canister and shake off excess flour.

If you bake the shortbread immediately after making the dough, you can freeze the baked cookies for up to 8 months.

1. Place flour, cheese, butter and cayenne pepper in food processor; whir until mixture forms a ball. Lightly flour ball.

2. Between two sheets of waxed paper, roll dough out to 1/4-inch thickness. Use cookie cutter to make shapes. If dough is too soft to cut, refrigerate to firm. Place shortbread on baking sheet lined with parchment paper. *If freezing, see "to freeze" section below; otherwise proceed with Step 3.*

3. Preheat oven to 350° F (180° C). Bake for 8 to 10 minutes or until golden. Serve warm or at room temperature.

VARIATIONS

Olive Cheese Shortbread: A third cup (75 mL) chopped pimento-stuffed olives may be incorporated into the dough before rolling out.

Seeded Cheese Shortbread: Brush rolled cookies with egg wash and sprinkle with poppyseeds or sesame seeds before baking, either before freezing or just before baking.

Blue-Cheese Nut Shortbread: Substitute 1 cup (250 mL) crumbled blue cheese for Cheddar. At end of Step 2, form into a log 8 inches (20 cm) long. Roll in 1/2 cup (125 mL) finely chopped walnuts or pecans. Wrap well in plastic. Chill until firm. Cut into 1/4-inch (5 mm) slices, place on baking sheet and freeze. (Alternatively, freeze in log form and cut slices from frozen log with sharp knife before baking; let thaw about 15 minutes before slicing.) Bake as above.

To freeze: Cover baking sheet with plastic wrap, then foil; seal, label and date. Freeze for up to 8 months.

To serve: Bake from frozen. Proceed with Step 3, above, increasing baking time to 14 to 16 minutes.

Pâté-Stuffed Baguette

MAKES ABOUT 24 PIECES

This is a different way to serve a smooth, flavorful pâté.

1/2 cup	unsalted butter	125 mL
1 cup	chopped onions	250 mL
1 cup	chopped peeled apple	250 mL
1 lb	chicken livers	500 g
1	bay leaf	1
1 tsp	salt	5 mL
1/2 tsp	dried thyme leaves	2 mL
1/2 tsp	dried marjoram	2 mL
1/2 tsp	black pepper	2 mL
1	pkg (8 oz [250 g]) cream cheese, softened	1
2 to 4 tbsp	dry sherry or brandy	25 to 50 mL
1	baguette	1

1. In a heavy frying pan, melt butter over medium-high heat. Add onions and apple; cook for 5 minutes or until softened. Stir in livers, bay leaf, salt, thyme, marjoram and pepper; cook for 6 minutes or until livers are browned outside but still pink in the center.

2. Remove bay leaf and discard. Spoon mixture into food processor; purée. Add cream cheese and 2 tbsp (25 mL) sherry; purée until smooth. Add additional sherry to taste. Adjust salt and pepper to taste. Spoon into bowl. Cover and chill until firm.

3. Cut baguette in half horizontally. Scoop out bread, leaving 1/2-inch (1 cm) shell of bread. Pack cavity with pâté. Put two halves back together. (Any extra pâté can be transferred to a freezer container and frozen for up to 2 months; thaw, stirring to smooth, before serving.)

To freeze: Wrap tightly in plastic wrap, over wrap with heavy foil.; seal, label and date. Freeze for up to 2 months.

To serve: Thaw wrapped baguette at room temperature for 3 hours. Cut into 3/4-inch (2 cm) pieces and arrange on serving platter.

Christmas Pissaladière

**MAKES ABOUT
3 TO 4 DOZEN
PIECES**

The French equivalent to
pizza, this version looks
festive with the green of the
peppers and olives against
the red tomato
background.

1 1/2 lbs	store-bought pizza dough	750 g
1/3 cup	grated Parmesan cheese	75 mL
Half	recipe Mediterranean Tomato Sauce (see page 135)	Half
2	green peppers, cut in 1/4-inch (5 mm) strips	2
1 cup	large pimento-stuffed olives, sliced	250 mL

1. On lightly floured counter, roll pizza dough out to fit baking sheet. Sprinkle dough with Parmesan cheese. Spread tomato sauce evenly over top. Sprinkle green peppers and olives over surface of pizza.

2. Bake in center of preheated oven for 30 to 35 minutes or until crust is golden.

To freeze: Cool to room temperature. Wrap tightly in plastic wrap, then overwrap with heavy foil; seal, label and date. Freeze for up to 2 months.

To serve: Thaw in refrigerator overnight. Serve at room temperature or warm (about 20 minutes in a preheated 350° F [180° C] oven). Cut into fingers and arrange on serving platter.

Mediterranean Tomato Sauce

**MAKES ABOUT
4 CUPS (1 L)**

This basic tomato sauce
may be tossed with pasta,
used as a savory pie filling,
a sauce for veal or chick-
en, or a topping for pizza,
such as Christmas
Pissaladière (see recipe,
page 134).

1/4 cup	butter	50 mL
1/4 cup	olive oil	50 mL
4 cups	chopped onions	1 L
3	cloves garlic, minced	3
1	can (28 oz [796 mL]) crushed tomatoes	1
2 tsp	dried thyme leaves	10 mL
1 tsp	dried basil	5 mL
1 tsp	dried rosemary	5 mL
	Salt and freshly ground black pepper	

1. In stainless steel saucepan, melt butter with oil over medium heat. Add onions and garlic; cook for 10 minutes or until softened.

2. Stir in tomatoes, thyme, basil and rosemary. Bring to a boil, reduce heat to simmer and cook 15 to 20 minutes or until mixture is thickened. Season to taste with salt and pepper.

To freeze: Cool to room temperature. Divide between 2 rigid freezer containers; seal, label and date. Freeze for up to 2 months.

To serve: Defrost in microwave or in refrigerator overnight. Reheat as required

Easy Bouillabaisse

SERVES 4 TO 6

This fish stew, originally from Provence, makes a wonderful dinner party dish. It never ceases to please, yet can be prepared with a minimum of fuss. The fish and seafood can be varied with personal preferences.

TIP

If you have leftovers with seafood in it, you can freeze it for up to 2 months; the texture of the fish and seafood will not be as nice. For entertaining, be sure to add fish and seafood just before serving.

For those people with seafood allergies, use additional fish to replace the shellfish in recipe.

2 tbsp	olive oil	25 mL
2	leeks, white part only, chopped	2
2	stalks celery, chopped	2
2	cloves garlic, crushed	2
1	onion, chopped	1
1	can (28 oz [796 mL]) diced tomatoes	1
1 cup	fish or chicken stock (see pages 70 and 69 for recipes)	250 mL
1 cup	dry white wine	250 mL
1	bay leaf	1
1	3-inch (8 cm) piece orange zest	1
1/2 tsp	ground fennel	2 mL
1/2 tsp	dried thyme leaves	2 mL
Pinch	cayenne pepper	Pinch
AFTER FREEZING/BEFORE SERVING		
1 lb	firm-fleshed fish such as cod, haddock, halibut or sea bass	500 g
8 oz	scallops	250 g
8 oz	shrimp	250 g
8 oz	mussels	250 g
1/2 cup	chopped fresh parsley	125 mL
2 tbsp	Pernod or other licorice-flavored liqueur (optional)	25 mL
	Salt and freshly ground black pepper	

1. In a large saucepan, heat oil over medium-high heat. Add leeks, celery, garlic and onion; cook for 5 minutes or until softened.

2. Stir in tomatoes and juices, stock, wine, bay leaf, orange zest, fennel, thyme and cayenne. Bring to a boil. Reduce heat, cover and simmer for 20 minutes. Remove from heat. *If freezing, see "to freeze" section below; otherwise proceed with Step 3.*

3. Cut fish into 1-inch (2 cm) cubes. In a saucepan bring soup to a boil. Add fish, scallops, shrimp and mussels. Reduce heat and simmer, uncovered, for about 5 minutes or until fish flakes easily with a fork. Discard any mussels that have not opened during cooking. Stir in parsley and, if using, Pernod. Season to taste with salt and pepper. Discard bay leaf and orange zest. Ladle into soup bowls. Serve with crusty bread.

To freeze: Cool to room temperature. Ladle into freezer container; seal, label and date. Freeze for up to 4 months.

To serve: Thaw in refrigerator overnight. Proceed with Step 3, above.

Mushroom Soup with Puff Pastry Dome

PREHEAT OVEN TO 400° F (200° C)
SIX OVENPROOF SOUP BOWLS, EACH ABOUT 4 INCHES (10 CM) WIDE AT TOP

SERVES 6

Imagine serving your guests bowls of fragrant mushroom soup capped by domes of golden puff pastry. You can almost hear the gasps of surprise!

For an elegant presentation, place bowls on underplates that are lined with large linen napkins folded in quarters.

You'll not want to be fiddling with this soup when your guests arrive, so make the mushroom and vegetable stock early in the day (or the day before) and refrigerate. Assemble the soups with their puff pastry domes in the late afternoon and chill. Just make sure that when you bake the soups in the oven, the liquid gets hot. If the pastry domes seem to be browning too quickly, cover each loosely with a piece of aluminum foil and continue baking.

From Marilyn Crowley and Joan Mackie, *The Best Soup Cookbook*

1 lb	mixed mushrooms (such as shiitake, cremini, oyster, chanterelle and portobello)	500 g
6 cups	chicken stock	1.5 L
8 oz	button mushrooms, sliced	250 g
2 tbsp	butter	25 mL
1	leek, white and light green parts only, sliced	1
1	carrot, julienned or finely diced	1
1	stalk celery, julienned or finely diced	1
1/2 tsp	salt	2 mL
1/4 tsp	black pepper	1 mL

AFTER FREEZING/BEFORE SERVING

1	pkg (14 oz [397 g]) frozen puff pastry, defrosted overnight in refrigerator	1
1	egg, lightly beaten	1

1. Wipe mixed mushrooms with a paper towel. Trim mixed mushrooms, reserving trimmings and stems; slice mushrooms caps thinly and set aside. In a large saucepan, combine reserved trimmings and stems with stock and button mushrooms; bring to a boil. Reduce heat and simmer, covered, for 20 minutes. Place a cheesecloth-lined sieve over a bowl; strain broth, discarding solids. Return broth to saucepan and set aside.

2. In a large skillet, melt butter over medium-high heat. Add leek, carrot, celery and sliced mixed mushrooms; sauté, stirring frequently, for 1 to 2 minutes or until just hot. Add to broth in saucepan; bring to a boil. Reduce heat and simmer for 5 minutes. Stir in salt and pepper. Taste and adjust seasonings as needed. *If freezing, see "to freeze" section on the next page; otherwise proceed with Steps 3 to 5.*

3. Puff pastry lids: Roll out pastry thinly (to about 1/8 inch [3 mm] thick). Using an inverted soup bowl as a guide, cut 6 circles of pastry, each 1 1/2 inches (4 cm) larger in diameter than the bowl.

4. Ladle soup into bowls until three-quarters full. Brush egg over rim and 1/2 inch (1 cm) down outer side of bowl; brush both sides of pastry. Without stretching, place circles on top of bowls; press firmly to bowl rims and sides. Set bowls on a baking sheet; refrigerate uncovered for 20 minutes – or, lightly covered, for up to half a day.

5. About half an hour before serving, transfer bowls on baking sheet directly from refrigerator to preheated oven; bake for 10 minutes. Reduce heat to 375° F (190° C); bake for an additional 15 to 20 minutes or until pastry is nicely browned. Serve immediately.

To freeze: Cool. Ladle into freezer containers. Seal, label and date. Freeze for up to 4 months.

To serve: Thaw soup in microwave or in refrigerator overnight. Proceed with Steps 3 to 5, above.

Leek Soufflé

Soufflés are one of the ultimate versatile dishes. They can be an appetizer, main course or dessert; they can use up bits and pieces of leftovers with an air of sophistication. They are quick and easy to make and can be extended to serve an extra guest simply by increasing the egg whites. And, they taste marvelous!

TIP

To clean leeks, slice in half lengthwise. Rinse under cold running water to clean between layers.

SIX 3/4-CUP (175 mL) RAMEKINS OR CUSTARD CUPS SPRAYED WITH VEGETABLE SPRAY

3 tbsp	butter	45 mL
2	small leeks, white parts only, thinly sliced	2
3 tbsp	all-purpose flour	45 mL
3/4 cup	milk	175 mL
3	eggs, separated	3
1/2 cup	shredded old Cheddar or Swiss cheese	125 mL
1/4 tsp	salt	1 mL
1/8 tsp	freshly ground black pepper	0.5 mL
1/8 tsp	ground nutmeg	0.5 mL
Pinch	cayenne pepper	Pinch
1	egg white	1
1 tbsp	grated Parmesan cheese	15 mL

1. In a heavy saucepan, melt butter over medium heat. Add leeks and cook, covered, for 5 minutes or until softened. Sprinkle with flour. Cook, stirring, until mixture begins to pull away from pan. Remove saucepan from heat. Gradually whisk in milk. Return to medium heat; cook, stirring, for 3 minutes or until thickened and bubbly. Remove from heat. Whisk in egg yolks, cheese, salt, pepper, nutmeg and cayenne. Transfer to a large bowl. Cool.

2. In a large clean bowl, beat all 8 egg whites until stiff peaks form. Stir one-quarter of egg whites into leek mixture. Gently fold in remaining egg whites.

3. Sprinkle bottom of prepared ramekins with half of Parmesan. Divide leek mixture evenly among ramekins. Sprinkle with remaining Parmesan. *If freezing, see "to freeze" section below; otherwise proceed with Step 4.*

4. Preheat oven to 400° F (200° C). Place soufflés in center of oven. Bake for 15 to 20 minutes or until puffed and golden. Souffle should still be moist in center; do not overcook.

To freeze: Freeze uncovered to firm then cover with plastic wrap and over wrap with heavy foil; seal, label and date. Freeze for up to 1 month.

To serve: Bake from frozen. Proceed with Step 4, above, increasing baking time to 25 to 30 minutes.

Seafood en Papillote

SERVES 6

These mouth-watering packages can be made with your favorite fresh or frozen seafood or fish or a mixture of both. Individual servings can be assembled ahead in parchment paper or foil packages, refrigerated until ready to serve, then baked in the oven. This method is the ultimate in convenience for easy entertaining.

TIP

You can assemble these papillotes with frozen fish and seafood.

If you plan to freeze the packets once they are assembled, be sure to use either fresh or unthawed frozen fish and seafood (otherwise it will be thawed twice).

1 1/2 lbs	scallops or medium shelled deveined shrimp or fish (such as sole, halibut, salmon) cut into 4 oz (125 g) fillets	750 g
1/3 cup	butter, softened	75 mL
8	oil-packed sun-dried tomatoes, chopped	8
1	clove garlic, crushed	1
2 tbsp	chopped fresh dill	25 mL
1 tbsp	dried tarragon	15 mL

1. Cut 6 rectangles of parchment paper or foil, each 13 by 10 inches (33 by 25 cm). Fold each rectangle in half to create 6 1/2- by 10-inch (16 by 25 cm) rectangles. Cut a large half heart against the folded edge so that when paper or foil is opened, you will have a large heart.

2. Arrange equal portions of fish or seafood on one half of each heart. In small bowl, beat butter, sun-dried tomatoes, garlic, dill and tarragon until well combined. Divide mixture evenly among portions, placing on top of fish or seafood.

3. If using parchment paper, beat an egg white and brush around outside edges of paper. Fold half of heart up and over filling, pressing curved edges of heart together. Double fold along curved edge. Place on baking sheet. *If freezing, see "to freeze" section below; otherwise proceed with Step 4.*

4. Preheat oven to 450° F (230° C). Bake in center of oven for 12 to 25 minutes (depending on whether fish and seafood are fresh or frozen), or until fish flakes easily, shrimp are pink or scallops are opaque. Place packages on heated dinner plates to be opened at the table.

To freeze: Overwrap sheet with heavy foil; seal, label and date. Freeze for up to 6 weeks.

To serve: Bake from frozen. Proceed with Step 4, above, baking 20 to 25 minutes.

Light 'n' Easy Chicken Tourtiere

SERVES 6 TO 8

This is a lighter version than the traditional pork tourtiere, using lower-fat ground chicken or turkey. Instead of a full pastry top, use Christmas cookie cutters to make pastry designs across the surface.

PASTRY

2 cups	all-purpose flour	500 mL
1/2 tsp	salt	2 mL
3/4 cup	shortening at room temperature	175 mL
1/3 cup	cold water	75 mL

FILLING

2 lbs	ground chicken or turkey or a combination	1 kg
1 1/2 cups	chopped onions	375 mL
2	cloves garlic, minced	2
1 to 1 1/2 cups	chicken stock	250 to 375 mL
1/2 cup	dry bread crumbs	125 mL
1/2 cup	finely chopped fresh parsley	125 mL
1/2 tsp	salt	2 mL
1/2 tsp	dried thyme leaves	2 mL
1/4 tsp	ground cloves	1 mL
1/4 tsp	ground nutmeg	1 mL
1/4 tsp	ground sage	1 mL
1/4 tsp	black pepper	1 mL

1. **Pastry**: In a bowl stir together flour and salt. Using pastry blender or two knives, cut in shortening until fine crumb consistency. Using a fork, stir in water. Form dough into a ball. Divide two-thirds, one-third into two balls. Wrap one-third portion in plastic wrap and refrigerate.

2. Place two-thirds portion of dough on sheet of waxed paper. Flatten slightly with heel of your hand. Place another sheet of waxed paper on top of dough. Gripping ends of waxed paper between your body and the counter, roll dough out to circle 1/2-inch (1 cm) larger than pie plate, turning waxed paper to roll in different directions.

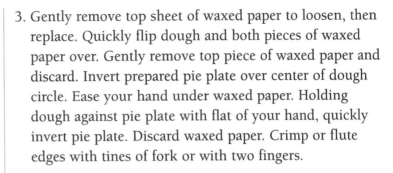

3. Gently remove top sheet of waxed paper to loosen, then replace. Quickly flip dough and both pieces of waxed paper over. Gently remove top piece of waxed paper and discard. Invert prepared pie plate over center of dough circle. Ease your hand under waxed paper. Holding dough against pie plate with flat of your hand, quickly invert pie plate. Discard waxed paper. Crimp or flute edges with tines of fork or with two fingers.

4. **Filling**: Preheat oven to 425° F (220° C). In large frying pan set over medium-high heat, cook chicken and/or turkey for 5 to 8 minutes or until browned, stirring to break meat up. Drain off any fat. Stir in onions and garlic; cook 5 minutes or until softened. Stir in 1 cup (250 mL) stock, bread crumbs, parsley, salt, thyme, cloves, nutmeg, sage and pepper. Cook for 5 to 10 minutes or until thickened. Stir in remaining stock, if desired, for a moister filling. Cool.

5. Between two sheets of waxed paper, roll remaining pastry to 1/8 inch (3 mm) thickness. Using cookie cutters, cut out desired shapes.

6. Spoon filling into pie shell. Place pastry shapes on top. Bake in center of oven for 30 to 35 minutes or until golden brown.

To freeze: Cool to room temperature. Wrap well with plastic wrap, then over wrap with foil; seal, label and date. Freeze for up to 1 month.

To serve: Thaw in microwave or overnight in refrigerator. Preheat oven to 350° F (180° C). Unwrap thawed pie and bake for 30 minutes or until hot. Serve warm or at room temperature.

Bittersweet Chocolate Truffles

One of the easiest little
gems to make. You can
never have enough truffles!
For best results, use top
quality imported chocolate.

TIP

To speed up the thickening
process, instead of letting
chocolate mixture stand at
room temperature for
2 hours, place bowl in
larger bowl of ice. The
chocolate should be well-
chilled and thickened
within an hour.

1 lb	imported bittersweet chocolate, chopped	500 g
1/2 cup	butter	125 mL
1/2 cup	whipping (35%) cream	125 mL
1/4 cup	orange-flavored liqueur or brandy or rum or whisky	50 mL
	Unsweetened cocoa powder	

1. In heatproof bowl set over a saucepan of simmering (not boiling) water, melt chocolate with butter. Stir in whipping cream. Set bowl on wire rack to cool.

2. Stir in liqueur. Let stand about 2 hours or until chocolate mixture is thick but not stiff.

3. Sift some cocoa into a small bowl. Take a heaped teaspoonful chocolate mixture and roll into a ball. Roll in cocoa. Repeat with remaining chocolate and cocoa.

To freeze: Store in tightly sealed plastic container; seal, label and date. Freeze for up to 2 months.

To serve: Thaw in truffle papers on counter for about 20 minutes. Serve at room temperature.

Chocolate Truffle Torte

SERVES 8 TO 12

To say that this is chocolate overload is an understatement! Serve this rich dessert in thin slivers accompanied by a dollop of whipped cream.

1 lb	imported bittersweet chocolate, chopped	500 g
1/2 cup	butter	125 mL
1/3 cup	Amaretto, Grand Marnier, rum or brandy	75 mL
1 cup	whipping (35%) cream	250 mL
1 cup	crumbled Amaretti cookies (about 20 cookies)	250 mL
1 cup	whipping (35%) cream	250 mL
1/4 cup	confectioner's (icing) sugar (optional)	50 mL
1 tbsp	Amaretto, Grand Marnier, rum or brandy (optional)	15 mL

1. In a bowl set over (not in) a saucepan of simmering (not boiling) water, melt chocolate with butter. Remove bowl from saucepan. Cool to room temperature. Stir in Amaretto.

2. In a bowl, beat whipping cream until stiff peaks form. Fold into cooled chocolate mixture. Sprinkle amaretti crumbs over bottom of prepared pan. Pour in chocolate mixture. Cover and refrigerate until firm.

3. Remove springform side. Slide torte, crumb-side down, onto serving platter. In a bowl, beat whipping cream with confectioner's sugar, if desired, until stiff peaks form. Beat in Amaretto. Pipe rosettes around base of torte, if desired, or simply serve a dollop of whipped cream on each plate.

To freeze: Wrap well with plastic, then over wrap with heavy foil; seal, label and date. Freeze for up to 4 months.

To serve: This torte can be sliced and served from frozen. But for best flavor, thaw on counter for 1 hour before serving.

Pear-Mincemeat Strudel

Large baking sheet lined with parchment paper

An easy but impressive dessert, rich with the flavors of pear and ginger; it also freezes well.

Tip

Instead of freezing raw and baking later, you can bake right away and freeze for up to 4 months. Thaw. Reheat in 350° F (180° C) oven for 15 minutes to crisp.

6	large Bosc or Bartlett pears, peeled, cored and sliced	6
1 cup	raisins	250 mL
3/4 cup	granulated sugar	175 mL
3/4 cup	chopped pecans	175 mL
3/4 cup	fine dry bread crumbs (made from French bread)	175 mL
1/2 cup	diced crystallized ginger Finely grated zest and juice of 1 lemon	125 mL
1/4 cup	rum or brandy	50 mL
1 tsp	ground cinnamon	5 mL
1/2 tsp	ground ginger	2 mL
1/2 tsp	ground nutmeg	2 mL
1	pkg (1 lb [500 g]) frozen phyllo pastry, thawed	1
3/4 cup	unsalted butter, melted	175 mL

After freezing/before serving

Confectioner's (icing) sugar

1. In a bowl combine pears, raisins, sugar, pecans, bread crumbs, crystallized ginger, lemon zest and juice, rum, cinnamon, ginger and nutmeg.

2. Layer 5 or 6 sheets of phyllo one on top the other, brushing each with butter as you stack them. Spoon one-third of pear mixture onto short end of dough. Fold about 1-inch (2 cm) of phyllo in along both long sides. Starting at pear filling end, roll up. Place on prepared baking sheet. Repeat with remaining filing, phyllo and butter. Brush strudels with remaining melted butter.

3. Using sharp knife, diagonally score strudels at 1-inch (2 cm) intervals, cutting three-quarter of the way through. *If freezing, see "to freeze" section below; otherwise proceed with Step 4.*

4. Preheat oven to 400° F (200° C). Unwrap strudels and bake in center of oven for 30 to 35 minutes or until golden. Sift confectioner's sugar over strudels and serve.

To freeze: Wrap well with plastic, then over wrap with heavy foil; seal, label and date. Freeze for up to 2 months.

To serve: Thaw in refrigerator overnight. Proceed with Step 4, above.

Cinnamon Chocolate Torte

PREHEAT OVEN TO 375° F (190° C)

THREE 9-INCH (1.5 L) ROUND CAKE PANS LINED WITH PARCHMENT PAPER

SERVES 12 TO 16

This cookie torte is worthy of a special occasion. It is divine!

TIP

Whipped cream freezes well because of its high fat content.

1 1/2 cups	butter, softened	375 mL
1 1/2 cups	granulated sugar	375 mL
2	eggs	2
3 cups	all-purpose flour	750 mL
2 tbsp	cinnamon	25 mL
FILLING		
1 cup	whipping (35%) cream	250 mL
3 tbsp	unsweetened cocoa powder	45 mL
2 cups	sour cream	500 mL
1/2 cup	grated semi-sweet chocolate	125 mL
1/2 cup	granulated sugar	125 mL
	Additional curls semi-sweet chocolate for garnish	

1. In a bowl, beat butter with sugar until light and fluffy. Beat in eggs one at a time.

2. In another bowl, stir together flour and cinnamon. With a wooden spoon, stir into butter mixture until smooth. Divide dough into 8 or 9 equal portions. Spread one portion into each prepared pan.

3. Bake in center of oven for 8 to 12 minutes or until golden brown. Cool cookies in pans on racks. Re-line pans with parchment and bake remaining dough in same manner.

4. **Filling**: In a bowl whip cream until stiff. Sift cocoa; fold into whipped cream. In another bowl, stir sugar into sour cream for 3 minutes or until sugar dissolves; stir in grated chocolate. Fold sour cream mixture into whipped cream mixture.

5. **Assembly**: Arrange one cookie on cake plate; spread with about one-eighth or ninth of filling. Continue to layer cookies and filling. Spread top cookie with remaining filling; make decorative swirls in cream. Garnish with a pile of chocolate curls.

To freeze: Poke several toothpicks in top of torte around outside edge. Wrap well with plastic wrap, then overwrap with heavy foil; seal, label and date. Freeze for up to 2 months.

To serve: Thaw on counter 1 hour before serving, or in refrigerator for 4 hours. Unwrap and remove toothpicks before serving.

baking

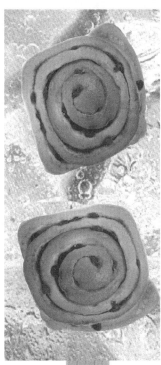

Preserving the baker's bounty

A freezer is a baker's best friend. Cookies, muffins, breads, both quick and yeast breads, cakes, squares and pies freeze extremely well. Baked goods are often frozen after baking. However, some recipes (such as refrigerator doughs for cookies or yeast bread, some batters and pies) freeze well when uncooked. This allows you to do most of the preparation work ahead of time, freeze, and end up with a "fresh baked" result. Freezing is also great for preserving the quality of baking ingredients. Whole grain flours, natural bran and wheat germ are kept fresh and free from insects in the freezer. Nuts, dried fruits, chocolate and maple syrup also benefit from freezing. Don't forget to freeze bananas whole with skins on. Even though they turn black in the freezer, once thawed, they can be mashed and used for cakes, loaves, cookies and ice-cream.

As with any type of frozen food, baked goods need to be properly prepared and packaged. Wrap tightly in airtight moisture-proof wrap, freezer containers or freeze in baking container overwrapped with heavy aluminum foil. Date, label and freeze up to the specified maximum storage time. Tips for specific types of baked goods are given below.

BISCUITS, MUFFINS, COFFEE CAKE, FRUIT BREAD

PREPARATION: Bake as usual; cool completely. Do not frost or decorate. Cover tightly; wrap in heavy foil.
FREEZE UP TO: 8 months.
TO SERVE: Thaw in wrapping at room temperature 2 to 3 hours or reheat in foil at 350° F (180° C) oven 15 to 20 minutes or until warm.

BREAD (YEAST), ROLLS, SWEET ROLLS, LOAVES, COFFEE CAKE

PREPARATION: Cool baked bread completely. Do not frost or decorate. Wrap tightly in heavy-duty foil.
FREEZE UP TO: 8 months
TO SERVE: Unwrap; thaw at room temperature 2 to 3 hours. Reheat at 350° F (180° C) 15 to 20 minutes or until warm.

CAKES, GENERAL

PREPARATION: Cakes can be frozen either frosted or unfrosted. Buttercream freezes best. Do not use egg white frosting or custard fillings. Cool completely. Freeze frosted cake unwrapped for frosting to harden. Wrap cake in plastic wrap, overwrap in heavy duty foil. Place in pan or rigid containers to prevent crushing. For best results, freeze cake and frosting separately.
FREEZE UP TO: 4 to 6 months (unfrosted); 1 to 3 months (frosted)
TO SERVE: Thaw cake in wrapping at room temperature 2 to 3 hours. Frost and serve according to recipe.

CAKES, ANGEL FOOD, CHIFFON, SPONGE

PREPARATION: Bake thoroughly. Cool completely. Freeze frosted cakes before wrapping; do not

use egg white frosting. For unfrosted cakes, wrap in plastic wrap, overwrap in heavy foil and freeze. Store in pan or rigid containers to prevent crushing.
FREEZE UP TO: 4 to 6 months (unfrosted); 1 to 3 months (frosted)
TO SERVE: Thaw frosted or filled cakes wrapped in refrigerator overnight. For unfrosted cakes, unwrap and thaw in refrigerator.

CHEESECAKES

PREPARATION: Cool completely and wrap tightly with heavy foil.
FREEZE UP TO: 4 to 5 months; 2 months for cheesecakes containing egg yolks.
TO SERVE: Thaw wrapped in refrigerator 4 to 6 hours.

COOKIES, BAKED

PREPARATION: Cool completely. Package in heavy foil, moisture-proof paper or rigid container with 2 layers of waxed paper between cookies. Freeze frosted or decorated cookies unwrapped; wrap once frozen.
FREEZE UP TO: 8 months (unfrosted); 1 to 2 months (frosted)
TO SERVE: Thaw in containers at room temperature. Remove from containers and serve.

COOKIES, UNBAKED

PREPARATION: For refrigerator cookies, form dough into roll, slice if desired, and package in moisture- and vapor-resistant paper. For drop cookies, drop dough on sheet or just package bulk dough; wrap as described above.
FREEZE UP TO: 8 months
TO SERVE: Thaw dough in refrigerator. Firm cookie dough can be sliced before completely thawed and baked.

PIES, BAKED FRUIT, MINCE, NUT

PREPARATION: Cool baked pies rapidly. Freeze before packaging. Pies are easier to wrap

after freezing. Wrap in heavy foil.
FREEZE UP TO: 3 to 4 months
TO SERVE: Let stand at room temperature for about 15 minutes, then heat in 325° F (170° C) oven for about 45 minutes or until warm.

PIES, CHIFFON

PREPARATION: Refrigerate to set. Freeze, then wrap. Omit whipped topping.
FREEZE UP TO: 1 to 2 months
TO SERVE: Unwrap; thaw in refrigerator for 2 to 3 hours. Top as desired.

PIES, UNBAKED FRUIT, MINCE, NUT

NOTE: Unbaked fruit pies have a better fresh-fruit flavor than frozen baked pies, but bottom crust tends to get soggy.
PREPARATION: Make as usual except add 1 extra tbsp (15 mL) flour or tapioca or 1/2 tbsp (7 mL) cornstarch to juicy fillings to prevent boiling over when pies are baked later. Do not cut vents in top crust. Cover with inverted foil plate, wrap tightly with heavy foil.
FREEZE UP TO: 2 to 3 months
TO SERVE: Unwrap and cut vent holes in upper crust. Put pan on cookie sheet. Bake without thawing at 450° F (230° C), 15 to 20 minutes. Reduce heat to 375° F (190° C) for 30 to 45 minutes or until top crust is brown and center is bubbly.

WAFFLES, PANCAKES, CREPES, FRENCH TOAST

PREPARATION: Cook to a light brown. Separate with waxed paper in layers in plastic container and then package.
FREEZE UP TO: 2 months
TO SERVE: Heat waffles and French toast in the toaster until hot and crispy. Thaw and heat crepes, pancakes and French toast, uncovered, 15 to 20 minutes at 350° F (180° C) or until warm.

Basic White Bread

MAKES 3 LOAVES

This recipe is the basis for many bread recipes. Instead of making three standard loaves, braid one-third (see variation below), make a Rolled Loaf with another third (see page 160) and use the final third to make a Swedish Tea Ring (see page 161).

TIP

It is not advisable to freeze raw dough and then bake, as the yeast can be killed and the end result will not be as good.

For any bread you can brush an egg wash on before baking to get a golden sheen. Beat one egg with 1 tbsp (5 mL) water.

VARIATIONS

BASIC WHOLE WHEAT BREAD: Decrease all-purpose flour to 4 1/2 cups (1.125 L) and add 4 1/2 cups (1.125 L) whole wheat flour.

BRAIDED LOAF: Instead of shaping into a loaf and placing in loaf pan, roll one-third of dough into a 15- by 5-inch (38 by 12 cm) rectangle. With sharp knife, cut each lengthwise into three equal strips. Starting at far end, braid the three strips together. Tuck ends under. Place three braided loaves on large greased baking sheet. Beat an egg with 1 tbsp 15 mL) water; brush over loaves. Sprinkle with 2 tbsp (25 mL) poppy or sesame seeds. Cover and let stand in warm place for 45 minutes or until doubled in bulk. Bake at 400° F (200° C) for about 25 minutes. Makes 1 braided loaf.

1 cup	lukewarm water	250 mL
2 tbsp	traditional active dry yeast	25 mL
1 tsp	granulated sugar	5 mL
2 cups	lukewarm water	500 mL
1/2 cup	granulated sugar	125 mL
1/2 cup	vegetable oil	125 mL
1 tbsp	salt	15 mL
9 cups	all-purpose flour (approx)	2.25 L

1. Rinse a large bowl with hot tap water to warm it. Pour 1 cup (250 mL) lukewarm water into bowl. Sprinkle with yeast and 1 tsp (5 mL) sugar. Let stand for 10 minutes or until frothy.

2. Whisk 2 cups (500 mL) water, 1/2 cup (125 mL) sugar, oil and salt into frothy yeast mixture. Whisk in enough flour, 1 cup (250 mL) at a time, to form a stiff batter. With a wooden spoon, stir in remaining flour, 1 cup (250 mL) at a time. Turn dough out onto lightly floured work surface. Flour hands and knead for 5 minutes or until dough is smooth and satiny. Place in clean, oiled bowl. Cover and let stand in warm place for 1 1/2 to 2 hours or until doubled in bulk.

3. Punch dough down. Divide dough into three equal portions. Shape into three loaves. Place each in prepared loaf pans. Cover and let stand in warm place for 1 hour or until doubled in bulk. Meanwhile, preheat oven to 400° F (200° C).

4. Bake loaves in center of oven for 30 to 35 minutes or until golden brown and firm to the touch. Cool in pans on wire rack 10 minutes. Remove from pans.

To freeze: When completely cool, wrap tightly in plastic wrap, then overwrap with heavy foil; seal, label and date. Freeze for up to 8 months.

To serve: Unwrap; thaw at room temperature 2 to 3 hours. Reheat at 350° F (180° C) 15 to 20 minutes or until warm.

Easy Health Bread

MAKES 2 LOAVES

Try this quickly made batter bread toasted with preserves at breakfast and keep one in the freezer ready to slice for sandwiches.

TIP

You can sprinkle extra seeds on top of dough after you spoon it into the loaf pan.

3 cups	lukewarm water	750 mL
2 tbsp	traditional active dry yeast	25 mL
2 tsp	granulated sugar	10 mL
1/4 cup	molasses or liquid honey	50 mL
1/4 cup	vegetable oil	50 mL
1 cup	natural bran	250 mL
1 cup	quick-cooking oats	250 mL
3/4 cup	skim milk powder	175 mL
1/2 cup	poppy seeds or sesame seeds or sunflower seeds	125 mL
1/4 cup	packed brown sugar	50 mL
1/4 cup	wheat germ (optional) or additional bran	50 mL
1 tbsp	salt	15 mL
6 cups	whole wheat flour	1.5 L

1. Rinse a large bowl with hot tap water to warm it. Pour lukewarm water into bowl. Sprinkle with yeast and sugar. Let stand for 10 minutes or until frothy.

2. Whisk in molasses, oil, bran, oats, milk powder, seeds, brown sugar, wheat germ (if using) and salt. Using wooden spoon, beat in flour 1 cup (250 mL) at a time. Beat vigorously until well-blended. Divide dough in half. Spoon into prepared pans, patting into shape. Cover and let stand in warm place for 45 minutes or until doubled in bulk.

3. Bake in center of preheated oven for 35 to 45 minutes or bread is golden and sounds hollow when tapped. Cool in pans on wire rack 10 minutes. Remove from pans.

To freeze: When completely cool, wrap tightly in plastic wrap, then over wrap with heavy duty foil; seal, label and date. Freeze for up to 8 months.

To serve: Unwrap; thaw at room temperature 2 to 3 hours. Reheat at 350° F (180° C) 15 to 20 minutes or until warm.

Sourdough Bread

MAKES 3 LOAVES

Traditionally, sourdough starters were made with the wild yeasts in the air. However, this method using commercial yeast produces a more consistent result. Once you have the starter on hand, you can use it for any number of recipes other than bread- cakes, pancakes, scones and muffins.

STARTER

1/2 cup	lukewarm water	125 mL
1 tbsp	traditional active dry yeast	15 mL
1 tsp	granulated sugar	5 mL
3 cups	all-purpose flour	750 mL
1 tbsp	granulated sugar	15 mL
1 tbsp	salt	15 mL
3 cups	lukewarm water	750 mL

FEEDER

2 cups	lukewarm water	500 mL
2 cups	all-purpose flour	500 mL

SOURDOUGH BREAD

1 cup	milk	250 mL
1/4 cup	granulated sugar	50 mL
2 tbsp	vegetable oil	25 mL
7 cups	all-purpose flour (approx)	1.75 L

EGG WASH

1	egg	1
1 tbsp	water	15 mL

1. **Starter**: Rinse a large bowl with hot tap water to warm it. Pour 1/2 cup (125 mL) lukewarm water into bowl. Sprinkle with yeast and 1 tsp (5 mL) sugar. Let stand for 10 minutes or until frothy.

2. Whisk in 3 cups (750 mL) flour, 1 tbsp (15 mL) sugar, salt and 3 cups (750 mL) water until smooth. Cover with plastic wrap. Let stand at room temperature for 3 days, stirring batter down once daily.

3. **Sourdough bread**: On the third day, grease three 8- by 4-inch (1.5 L) loaf pans. Heat milk until steaming. Place In a large bowl. Whisk in sugar and oil. Blend in 3 cups (750 mL) of the sourdough starter. To remaining

sourdough starter, whisk in 2 cups (500 mL) lukewarm water and 2 cups (500 mL) all-purpose flour; let stand at room temperature for 1 day, then pour into a glass container and store, covered, in the refrigerator to use for future bread making. (Feed starter once a week – discard or use half and to remainder add 1 cup [250 mL] each water and flour.)

4. To hot milk-sourdough starter mixture, 1 cup (250 mL) at a time, using wooden spoon, stir in approximately 7 cups (1.75 L) flour to form a heavy dough. You may not need all of flour. Turn out onto floured surface. Knead 5 minutes or until dough is smooth and elastic. Shape into a ball and place in a clean, oiled bowl. Cover and let stand in warm place for 1 hour 15 minutes or until doubled in bulk.

5. Punch dough down. Turn out onto floured surface. Knead for 2 minutes or until smooth and elastic. Divide dough into 3 equal portions. Shape into loaves and place in prepared loaf pans. Beat egg with water; brush over tops of loaves. Cover and let stand in warm place for 45 minutes or until doubled in bulk. Meanwhile, preheat oven to 400° F (200° C).

6. Bake in center of oven for 30 to 35 minutes or until loaves are golden brown and sound hollow when tapped. Cool in pans on wire rack 15 minutes. Remove from pans.

To freeze: When completely cool, wrap tightly in plastic wrap, then over wrap with heavy duty foil; seal, label and date. Freeze for up to 8 months.

To serve: Unwrap; thaw at room temperature 2 to 3 hours. Reheat at 350° F (180° C) 15 to 20 minutes or until warm.

Whole Wheat Cheese Scones

PREHEAT OVEN TO 425° F (220° C)
BAKING SHEET LINED WITH PARCHMENT PAPER

MAKES ABOUT 6 LARGE SCONES

Keep a batch of these in the freezer to add to lunches or to serve with soups or stews.

TIP

If you don't have any buttermilk, place 1 tsp (5 mL) vinegar in measuring cup and pour in milk to make 1/2 cup (125 mL).

Generally, you get a higher rise on most baked products if they are baked and then frozen. When frozen raw and then baked, baked goods do not rise as high.

Pop into your kids lunch boxes from the freezer, for breakfast on the run or a nutritious after school snack.

VARIATION

MINI-SCONES: Use 1 1/2 inch (4 cm) cookie cutter to make 12 small scones.

1 cup	whole wheat flour	250 mL
1 cup	all-purpose flour	250 mL
2 tsp	baking powder	10 mL
1/2 tsp	baking soda	2 mL
1/2 tsp	salt	2 mL
1/3 cup	shortening	75 mL
1 cup	coarsely shredded old Cheddar cheese	250 mL
1/2 cup	buttermilk	125 mL
1	egg	1

1. In a large bowl, stir together flours, baking powder, baking soda and salt. Using pastry blender or two knives, cut in shortening until fine crumb consistency. Stir in cheese.

2. In a measuring cup, stir together buttermilk and egg. Reserve 1 tbsp (15 mL) of this mixture. Make a well in center of flour mixture. Using a fork, stir in remaining buttermilk mixture just until moistened. Form dough into a ball. Pat into a circle about 7 inches (18 cm) in diameter and 1 1/2 (4 cm) inches high.

3. Using 2 1/2 inch (6 cm) cookie cutter, cut into 6 or 7 large scones. Place on prepared baking sheet. Brush with reserved buttermilk mixture. Bake in center of oven for 10 to 12 minutes or until golden. Cool.

To freeze: When completely cool, wrap individual scones tightly in plastic wrap, then over wrap with heavy duty foil; seal, label and date. Freeze for up to 8 months.

To serve: Unwrap; thaw at room temperature 2 to 3 hours. Reheat at 350° F (180° C) 15 to 20 minutes or until warm.

Whole Wheat Soda Bread

PREHEAT OVEN TO 375° F (190° C)
9- BY 5-INCH (2 L) LOAF PAN LINED WITH PARCHMENT PAPER
AND SPRAYED WITH BAKING SPRAY

MAKES 1 LOAF

This recipe is particularly appealing because it is so versatile – it is easy to make, uses no fat, is excellent toasted or served plain and is a delicious companion to soup and a salad. Chopped dried fruit may be added to make it more like a dessert tea bread.

TIP

Be sure to measure dry ingredients accurately by spooning into a dry measure and level off with the flat side of a knife.

2 cups	all-purpose flour	500 mL
1 cup	whole wheat flour	250 mL
1 cup	natural bran	250 mL
1 cup	quick-cooking oats	250 mL
1/4 cup	poppy seeds or sesame seeds or a combination	50 mL
2 tsp	baking powder	10 mL
1 tsp	baking soda	5 mL
1 tsp	salt	5 mL
1 1/2 cups	milk or a mixture of milk and plain yogurt	375 mL
1/3 cup	liquid honey or molasses	75 mL

1. In a large bowl, stir together flour, whole wheat flour, bran, oats, seeds, baking powder, baking soda and salt. Stir in milk and honey just until moistened. Spoon into prepared pan.

2. Bake in center of oven for 40 to 50 minutes or until tester inserted in center comes out clean.

3. Cool fully in pan on wire rack. Remove from pan. Discard parchment paper.

To freeze: When completely cool, wrap tightly in plastic wrap, then over wrap with heavy duty foil; seal, label and date. Freeze for up to 8 months.

To serve: Unwrap; thaw at room temperature 2 to 3 hours. Reheat at 350° F (180° C) 15 to 20 minutes or until warm.

Cornbread

MAKES 6 TO 8 WEDGES

Serve this moist cornbread with soups or salads. It is great packed for lunch too.

VARIATION

SPICY CORNBREAD: Omit peppers. Substitute 1/4 cup (50 mL) each diced jalapeno peppers and green onions.

9-INCH (1.5 L) ROUND CAKE PAN LINED WITH PARCHMENT PAPER
PREHEAT OVEN TO 375° F (190° C)

1/3 cup	shortening	75 mL
1/4 cup	granulated sugar	50 mL
1	egg	1
1 cup	cake and pastry flour	250 mL
1 cup	cornmeal	250 mL
2 tsp	baking powder	10 mL
1 tsp	baking soda	5 mL
1/2 tsp	salt	2 mL
1 cup	plain yogurt	250 mL
1/2 cup	milk	125 mL
1/4 cup	diced red bell peppers	50 mL
1/4 cup	diced green peppers	50 mL

1. In a bowl and using electric mixer, beat shortening, sugar and egg until fluffy. In another bowl, stir together flour, cornmeal, baking powder, baking soda and salt. In a third bowl, combine yogurt and milk. With wooden spoon, alternately stir flour mixture and yogurt mixture into shortening mixture, making two additions of dry and two of wet and stirring just until moistened. Stir in peppers. Spoon batter into prepared pan.

2. Bake cornbread in center of oven for about 45 minutes or top is golden and a cake tester inserted in center comes out clean. Turn out of pan onto wire rack. Remove parchment paper. Serve warm.

To freeze: Wrap with heavy foil; seal, label and date. Freeze for up to 8 months.

To serve: Unwrap; thaw at room temperature 2 to 3 hours. Reheat at 350° F (180° C) 15 to 20 minutes or until warm.

Focaccia

This savory Italian flatbread can be varied with the use of different herbs or by substituting whole wheat flour.

VARIATIONS

FOCACCIA PIZZA CRUST: Omit herbs, if desired. After baking for 15 minutes, top with one of the following, then continue to bake 5 to 10 minutes longer or until deep golden brown around the edges. Cool, wrap and freeze for up to 2 months.

YUPPIE PIZZA: Basil Pesto (see page 54) or Winter Pesto (see page 121), marinated artichoke hearts, sun-dried tomatoes, black olives and sweet red pepper

TRADITIONAL: Tomato sauce (see page 120 or page 135), a sprinkling of chopped fresh herbs and sliced mushrooms (any variety).

PROVENCAL: Ratatouille (see page 82) and freshly grated Parmesan cheese

CARAMELIZED ONION: In olive oil, cook sliced onions, leeks and chopped garlic over medium-low heat for 15 minutes or until very soft, sweet and browned. Spread over pizza base. Sprinkle with rosemary or sage; top with cheese, if desired.

1 cup	lukewarm water	250 mL
1 tbsp	traditional active dry yeast	15 mL
1 tsp	granulated sugar	5 mL
3 tbsp	olive oil	45 mL
2	cloves garlic, crushed	2
2 tbsp	dried herbs (such as basil, oregano, rosemary, sage or thyme or a combination or 1/4 cup (50 mL) chopped fresh herbs	25 mL
1 tsp	salt	5 mL
2 cups	all-purpose flour	500 mL
2 tsp	coarse salt	10 mL

1. Rinse a large bowl with hot tap water to warm it. Pour lukewarm water into bowl. Sprinkle with yeast and sugar. Let stand for 10 minutes or until frothy. Meanwhile, in frying pan, heat 2 tbsp (25 mL) of the oil over medium heat; cook garlic and herbs for 30 seconds, stirring, or until fragrant.

2. Whisk oil-herb mixture and salt into frothy yeast mixture. Gradually whisk in enough flour to form a stiff batter. Stir in enough flour to make a stiff dough. Turn out onto work surface. Knead in any remaining flour. Knead for about 3 minutes or until dough is smooth and springy to the touch. Place in clean, oiled bowl. Cover and let stand in warm place for 1 to 1 1/2 hours or until doubled in bulk.

3. Punch dough down. Shape into 12-inch (30 cm) circle on pizza pan. Poke indentations into dough with fingers. Brush with remaining olive oil. Sprinkle with coarse salt. Cover and let rise in warm place for 30 minutes.

4. Preheat oven to 425° F (220° C). Bake for 20 to 25 minutes or until deep golden brown around edges. Serve hot or at room temperature. Makes one 12-inch (30 cm) bread. Cool to room temperature.

To freeze: When completely cool, wrap tightly in plastic wrap, then over wrap with heavy foil; seal, label and date. Freeze for up to 8 months.

To serve: Unwrap; thaw at room temperature 2 to 3 hours. Reheat at 350° F (180° C) 15 to 20 minutes or until warm.

Herb-Filled Rolled Loaf

9- BY 5-INCH (2 L) LOAF PAN, GREASED

MAKES 1 LOAF

VARIATION

CHEESE-FILLED ROLLED LOAF:
Omit herb filling. Spread
dough rectangle with
1 tbsp (15 mL) Dijon mustard. Sprinkle evenly with
1 1/2 cups (375 mL)
shredded old Cheddar
cheese, 1/2 cup (125 mL)
grated Parmesan cheese
and 1 tsp (5 mL)
Worcestershire sauce. Form
loaf and bake as above.

Third	White Bread dough recipe (see page 152), completed to end of step 2	Third
1	egg	1
HERB FILLING		
1/4 cup	butter	50 mL
1 cup	chopped green onions	250 mL
1/2 cup	chopped fresh parsley	125 mL
1	clove garlic, minced	1
1 tbsp	lemon juice	15 mL
Pinch	salt	Pinch
Pinch	freshly ground black pepper	Pinch

1. **Herb Filling**: In a frying pan, melt butter over medium-high heat. Add green onions, parsley and garlic; cook 2 to 3 minutes. Remove from heat. Stir in lemon juice, salt and pepper. Cool.

2. Punch dough down. Roll bread dough into rectangle 1/4-inch (5 mm) thick, about 14 by 8 inches (35 by 20 cm). Spread with herb filling. Starting from short end, roll up. Tuck ends under. Place in prepared loaf pan. Cover and let stand in warm place for 1 1/2 hours or until doubled in bulk. Meanwhile, preheat oven to 400° F (200° C).

3. Beat egg together with 1 tbsp (15 mL) water. Brush egg wash over loaf. Bake in center of oven for 30 to 35 minutes or until golden and firm to the touch. Cool in pan on wire rack 10 minutes. Remove from pan.

To freeze: When completely cool, wrap tightly in plastic wrap, then over wrap with heavy foil; seal, label and date. Freeze for up to 8 months.

To serve: Unwrap; thaw at room temperature 2 to 3 hours. Reheat at 350° F (180° C) 15 to 20 minutes or until warm.

BIG-BATCH BRAN MUFFINS (PAGE 174) ➤
BANANA-BERRY WAKE-UP SHAKE (PAGE 64)

Swedish Tea Ring

BAKING SHEET LINED WITH PARCHMENT

MAKES 1 LOAF

Third	White Bread dough recipe (see page 152), completed to end of step 2	Third
2 tbsp	butter, softened	25 mL
1/2 cup	packed brown sugar	125 mL
1/2 cup	chopped nuts	125 mL
1/2 cup	raisins	125 mL
1 tsp	ground cinnamon	5 mL
1/2 tsp	ground nutmeg	2 mL
GLAZE		
3/4 cup	confectioner's (icing) sugar	175 mL
1 tbsp	lemon juice	15 mL

1. Roll bread dough into rectangle 1/4-inch (5 mm) thick, about 14 by 8 inches (35 by 20 cm). Spread with butter. Sprinkle with brown sugar, nuts, raisins, cinnamon and nutmeg.

2. Starting from long end, roll up. Form into a circle. Place on prepared baking sheet. With a sharp knife, slice almost all the way through ring at 1-inch (2.5cm) intervals, leaving it joined at the center. Separate slices, turning one slice up and one slice down all the way around ring. Cover and let stand in warm place for 1 hour or until doubled in bulk. Meanwhile, preheat oven to 400° F (200° C).

3. Bake in center of oven for 30 to 35 minutes or until golden brown. Cool to room temperature on wire rack.

4. **Glaze**: In small bowl, whisk confectioner's sugar with lemon juice until smooth. Drizzle over loaf decoratively.

To freeze: When completely cool, wrap tightly in plastic wrap, then over wrap with heavy foil; seal, label and date. Freeze for up to 8 months.

To serve: Unwrap; thaw at room temperature 2 to 3 hours. Reheat at 350° F (180° C) 15 to 20 minutes or until warm.

◄ CRANBERRY OATMEAL COOKIES (PAGE 175)

Short Crust Pastry

This recipe is for those of you who are pastry challenged. The technique of rolling between waxed paper ensures you can prepare tender, flaky pastry without a hassle!

TIP

If baking blind (i.e. without a filling), line with parchment paper and weight down with about 3 cups (750 mL) dried beans, rice or pie weights. Remove paper and weights when you reduce the heat.

If you have limited number of pie plates, after the crusts are frozen, pop them out of the pie plates and stack, separated by parchment paper; place in large rigid container and return to freezer.

For a top crust for a double crust pie, fill a frozen shell with filling. Invert a second frozen shell on top of the pie and pop it out of the pie plate. Press edges slightly and bake.

TWO 9-INCH (23 CM) PIE PLATES SPRAYED WITH BAKING SPRAY

2 cups	all-purpose flour	500 mL
1/2 tsp	salt	2 mL
3/4 cup	shortening, at room temperature	175 mL
1/3 cup	cold water	75 mL

1. In a bowl stir together flour and salt. Using pastry blender or two knives, cut shortening into flour mixture until fine crumb consistency. Using fork, stir water into mixture. Gather dough into a ball. Divide in half. Form each half into a ball.

2. Place a ball of dough on sheet of waxed paper. Flatten slightly with heel of your hand. Place another sheet of waxed paper on top of dough. Gripping ends of waxed paper between your body and the counter, roll dough out to circle 1/2-inch (1 cm) larger than pie plate, turning waxed paper to roll in different directions.

3. Gently remove top sheet of waxed paper to loosen, then replace. Quickly flip dough and both pieces of waxed paper over. Gently remove top piece of waxed paper and discard. Invert prepared pie plate over center of dough circle. Ease your hand under waxed paper. Holding dough against pie plate with flat of your hand, quickly invert pie plate. Discard waxed paper. Gently ease dough into pie shell. Trim dough. Patch edges with pastry scraps. Crimp or flute edges with tines of fork or with two fingers. Repeat with second ball of dough.

To freeze: Wrap with heavy foil; seal, label and date. Freeze for up to 2 months.

VARIATIONS

BUTTERY: For a richer, butter pastry suitable for fruit tartlets and some seafood pies, decrease shortening to 1/4 cup (50 mL) and add 1/2 cup (125 mL) butter.

WHOLE WHEAT: Use 1 cup (250 mL) all-purpose flour and 1 cup (250 mL) whole wheat flour.

MINI-TARTLET SHELLS: Cut pastry into 2 3/4-inch (7 cm) circles with round cutter and press into mini-muffin cups. Freeze. Once frozen, invert muffin tin to pop out frozen shells; stack and store in rigid container in freezer.

To serve: May be baked thawed or frozen. Preheat oven to 425° F (220° C). If thawing pastry and then baking, bake in center of oven for 15 minutes; reduce oven temperature to 350° F (180° C) and bake for 20 to 25 minutes longer for shell, or 40 to 45 minutes if filled. If baking from frozen, bake in center of oven for 15 minutes; reduce oven temperature to 375° F (190° C) and bake for 20 to 25 minutes or until pale golden brown for shell, or 40 to 45 minutes if filled.

Mock Puff Pastry

TWO 9-INCH (23 CM) PIE PLATES SPRAYED WITH BAKING SPRAY

2 cups	all-purpose flour	500 mL
1 tsp	baking powder	5 mL
1/2 tsp	salt	2 mL
3/4 cup	cold butter	175 mL
3/4 cup	sour cream	175 mL

1. In a large bowl, stir together flour, baking powder and salt. Using pastry blender or two knives, cut butter into flour mixture until coarse crumb consistency. Stir in sour cream. Form into a ball. Divide in half. Form each half into a ball. Wrap in plastic wrap. Refrigerate for 1 hour or until dough is firm enough to roll.

2. Place a ball of dough on sheet of waxed paper. Flatten slightly with heel of your hand. Place another sheet of waxed paper on top of dough. Gripping ends of waxed paper between your body and the counter, roll dough out to circle 1/8-inch (3 mm) thick, turning waxed paper to roll in different directions.

3. Gently remove top sheet of waxed paper to loosen, then replace. Quickly flip dough and both pieces of waxed paper over. Gently remove top piece of waxed paper and discard. Invert prepared pie plate over center of dough circle. Ease your hand under waxed paper. Holding dough against pie plate with flat of your hand, quickly invert pie plate. Discard waxed paper. Gently ease dough into pie shell. Trim dough. Patch edges with pastry scraps. Crimp or flute edges with tines of fork or with two fingers. Repeat with second ball of dough.

If you have limited number of pie plates, after the crusts are frozen, pop them out of the pie plates and stack, separated by parchment paper; place in large rigid container and return to freezer.

For a top crust for a double crust pie, fill a frozen shell with filling. Wet edges of pastry with water. Invert a second frozen shell on top of the pie and pop it out of the pie plate. Press edges slightly and bake.

VARIATIONS

CHEESE PUFF PASTRY: Stir 1/4 cup (50 mL) grated Parmesan cheese into flour mixture before cutting in butter. Freeze as above; use to top pot pies or cut into shapes before baking for a cheese pastry appetizer.

SOUP GARNISH CUT-OUTS: To make a garnish to serve with soups or stews, thaw pastry a few minutes to soften slightly, then cut pastry out with cookie cutters and bake at 425° F (220° C) about 15 minutes or until golden brown.

To freeze: Wrap with heavy foil; seal, label and date. Freeze for up to 2 months.

To serve: Preheat oven to 425° F (220° C). Bake from frozen in center of oven for 15 minutes; reduce oven temperature to 375° F (190° C) and bake for 20 to 25 minutes or until pale golden brown for shell, or 40 to 45 minutes if filled.

Cream Cheese Pastry

MAKES
2 PIE SHELLS

This is the best pastry for making fussy appetizer tartlets or turnovers because it is flexible and strong.

TIP

If dough seems sticky, dip into your flour canister and shake off excess flour. It should be just enough flour to keep the dough from sticking as you roll it out but not enough to toughen pastry.

VARIATION

Filled Turnover: Cut pastry into circles. Place sweet or savory filling on lower half of circle; fold in half, pressing edges together. Brush with egg wash (1 egg beaten with 1 tbsp (15 mL) water). Bake for about 20 minutes or until golden.

2 cups	all-purpose flour	500 mL
1/2 tsp	salt	2 mL
1 cup	cold butter, cubed	250 mL
1	pkg (8 oz [250 g]) cream cheese, cut into cubes	1

1. In a food processor, combine flour and salt. Add butter and cream cheese; using on/off switch, pulse dough until it forms a ball. Divide in two. Form each half into a ball. Lightly flour balls. If dough seems too moist to roll, wrap in plastic and chill for 1 hour or until firm enough to roll.

2. Place a ball of dough on sheet of waxed paper. Flatten slightly with heel of your hand. Place another sheet of waxed paper on top of dough. Gripping ends of waxed paper between your body and the counter, roll dough out to rectangle 1/8-inch (3 mm) thick, turning waxed paper to roll in different directions. Repeat with second ball of dough.

To freeze: Wrap with heavy foil; seal, label and date. Freeze for up to 2 months.

To serve: Preheat oven to 375° F (190° C). Thaw pastry slightly on counter until pliable. Cut pastry to fit tartlet molds. Fit into tartlet molds. Bake 20 minutes or until golden. Cool. Fill with filling of your choice.

Apple-Any Berry Pie

MAKES 2 PIES

A good old-fashioned classic. You can vary it with the berries of your choice.

TIP

Brush pastry bottom with egg white before filling with fruit to prevent pastry going soggy.

4 cups	sliced peeled apples	1 L
2 cups	berries (such as strawberries, raspberries or cranberries)	500 mL
1/2 cup	raisins or chopped nuts (optional)	125 mL
3/4 to 1 cup	granulated sugar (depending on sweetness of fruit)	175 to 250 mL
1 tsp	ground cinnamon	5 mL
1 tsp	finely grated orange or lemon zest	5 mL
1/2 cup	orange juice	125 mL
1 tbsp	cornstarch	15 mL

AFTER FREEZING/BEFORE SERVING

2	Short Crust Pastry pie shells, (9-inch [23 cm]), frozen or thawed (see recipe, page 162)	2

1. In a saucepan, combine apples, berries, raisins or nuts (if using), sugar, cinnamon, zest, orange juice and cornstarch. Cook over low heat about 10 minutes or until juices are clear and thickened. Cool. *If freezing, see "to freeze" section below; otherwise proceed with Step 2.*

2. Pour filling into 9-inch (23 cm) pastry lined shell.

3. Preheat oven to 425° F (220° C). Top filled shell with another piecrust. Crimp edges together. Brush with egg wash if desired.

4. Bake for 15 minutes. Reduce oven temperature to 350° F (180° C); bake another 40 to 45 minutes or until golden.

5. Pie may be served immediately or cooled and wrapped with plastic wrap and over wrapped with heavy foil.

To freeze: Transfer filling to 9 inch (23 cm) foil pie plate. Wrap with heavy foil; seal, label and date. Freeze for up to 3 to 4 months.

To serve: Pop frozen filling out of pie shell and slide into 9-inch (23 cm) pastry lined shell. Proceed with Steps 3 to 5, above.

Harvest Apple, Pear and Cranberry Pie with Cheddar Pastry

MAKES ONE 9-INCH (23 CM) PIE

Experiment with different apple and pear varieties when making this pie. Serve with a spoonful of homemade vanilla ice-cream for dessert perfection!

TIP

To give a frozen pie that "just baked flavor", warm it in a 350° F (180° C) oven for 20 minutes after thawing.

VARIATIONS

BUTTER CHEDDAR CRUST: Use 1/2 cup (125 mL) shortening and 1/4 cup (50 mL) butter instead of 3/4 cup (175 mL) shortening in the pastry.

•

PEAR AND APPLE TART: Omit cranberries. Increase pears to 3 cups (750 mL) and decrease flour to 2 tbsp (25 mL).

CHEDDAR PASTRY

2 cups	all-purpose flour	500 mL
1/2 tsp	salt	2 mL
3/4 cup	shortening	175 mL
1/3 cup	cold water	75 mL
1/2 cup	shredded old Cheddar cheese	125 mL

APPLE, PEAR AND CRANBERRY FILLING

1/3 cup	granulated sugar	75 mL
1/3 cup	packed brown sugar	75 mL
1/4 cup	all-purpose flour	50 mL
1 tsp	ground cinnamon	5 mL
1/2 tsp	ground nutmeg	2 mL
1/2 tsp	ground ginger	2 mL
4 cups	sliced peeled apples	1 L
2 cups	sliced peeled pears	500 mL
1 cup	cranberries	250 mL

1. **Cheddar Pastry**: In a bowl stir together flour and salt. Using a pastry blender or two knives, cut shortening into flour mixture until fine crumb consistency. Using a fork, stir in water and cheese. Gather dough into a ball. Divide in half. Form each half into a ball.

2. Place a ball of dough on sheet of waxed paper. Flatten slightly with heel of your hand. Place another sheet of waxed paper on top of dough. Gripping ends of waxed paper between your body and the counter, roll dough out to circle 1/2 inch (1 cm) larger than 9-inch (23 cm) pie plate, turning waxed paper to roll in different directions.

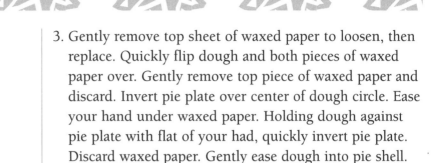

3. Gently remove top sheet of waxed paper to loosen, then replace. Quickly flip dough and both pieces of waxed paper over. Gently remove top piece of waxed paper and discard. Invert pie plate over center of dough circle. Ease your hand under waxed paper. Holding dough against pie plate with flat of your had, quickly invert pie plate. Discard waxed paper. Gently ease dough into pie shell. Trim dough. Patch edges with pastry scraps. Wrap remaining ball of dough and chill while making filling.

4. **Filling**: In a bowl stir together sugars, flour, cinnamon, nutmeg and ginger. Stir in apples, pears and cranberries until well blended. Spoon into pie shell.

5. Between two sheets of waxed paper, roll remaining ball of dough to 9-inch (23 cm) circle. Place on top of pie. Fold edges of top crust under edges of bottom crust; crimp or flute edges with tines or a fork or with two fingers.

6. Preheat oven to 425° F (220° C). Bake for 15 minutes. Reduce heat to 350° F (180° C); bake another 40 to 45 minutes or until golden. Cool to room temperature.

To freeze: When completely cool, wrap tightly in plastic wrap, then over wrap with heavy foil; seal, label and date. Freeze for up to 2 months.

To serve: Unwrap pie and let stand at room temperature about 15 minutes, then heat in 325° F (170° C) oven for about 45 minutes or until warm.

Macaroon Cake with Grand Marnier Glaze

PREHEAT OVEN TO 350° F (180° C)
10-INCH (4 L) TUBE PAN SPRAYED WITH BAKING SPRAY.

SERVES 16

This rich cake is wonderful with fresh berries. It makes enough to feed a crowd and leftovers freeze well for up to 6 months. For a glamorous presentation serve the cake on a cake stand with a small bouquet of flowers in the center of the cake and a few blossoms at the base.

1 cup	butter, softened	250 mL
2 cups	granulated sugar	500 mL
1 tbsp	finely grated lemon zest	15 mL
1 tbsp	finely grated orange zest	15 mL
6	eggs	6
1 tsp	almond extract	5 mL
3 cups	sweetened flaked coconut	750 mL
2 cups	all-purpose flour	500 mL
1 tsp	baking powder	5 mL
1/4 tsp	salt	1 mL

GRAND MARNIER GLAZE

1 cup	orange juice	250 mL
3/4 cup	granulated sugar	175 mL
2 tbsp	lemon juice	25 mL
2 tbsp	Grand Marnier	25 mL

1. In a large bowl using electric mixer, beat butter, sugar, lemon zest and orange zest until creamy. Beat eggs into creamed mixture one at a time until fluffy. Beat in almond extract.

2. In another bowl, stir together coconut, flour, baking powder and salt. With wooden spoon, stir into butter mixture, 1 cup (250 mL) at a time, stirring just until combined. Spoon batter into prepared pan.

3. Bake in center of oven 50 to 60 minutes or until cake tester inserted in center comes out clean. Cool in pan on wire rack 15 minutes. Turn out onto wire rack. Glaze while still warm.

4. Glaze: In a saucepan combine orange juice, sugar and lemon juice. Bring to a boil. Reduce heat and simmer uncovered for 10 minutes. Cool slightly. Stir in Grand Marnier before drizzling over warm cake. Cool cake fully.

To freeze: When completely cool, wrap tightly in plastic wrap, then over wrap with heavy foil; seal, label and date. Freeze for up to 6 months.

To serve: Thaw cake wrapped in refrigerator overnight.

Fruited, Freeze-Ahead Bran Muffins

12-CUP MUFFIN TIN AND ONE 6-CUP MUFFIN TIN LINED WITH.
LARGE PAPER MUFFIN LINERS

MAKES 18
MUFFINS

This versatile recipe can be made with the dried fruit of your choice. For ultimate convenience, the raw batter can be frozen then baked.

2 cups	natural bran	500 mL
2 cups	all-purpose flour	500 mL
1/2 cup	packed brown sugar	125 mL
1 1/2 tsp	baking soda	7 mL
1 tsp	ground cinnamon	5 mL
1 tsp	salt	5 mL
2	eggs	2
1	can (14 oz [385 mL]) 2% evaporated milk	1
1/2 cup	honey	125 mL
2/3 cup	vegetable oil	150 mL
1 cup	chopped dates, raisins or dried cranberries or combination	250 mL
1 tbsp	finely grated orange zest	15 mL

1. In a large bowl, stir together bran, all-purpose flour, brown sugar, baking soda, cinnamon and salt.

2. In another bowl, whisk together eggs, milk, honey and oil. Stir into bran mixture just until moistened. Stir in fruit and orange zest. Spoon evenly into prepared muffin cups. *If freezing, see "to freeze" section below; otherwise proceed with Step 3.*

3. Preheat oven to 400° F (200° C). Bake muffins in center of oven for 18 to 20 minutes or until firm to the touch.

To freeze: Wrap muffin cups with heavy foil; seal, label and date. Freeze for up to 1 month.

To serve: Can be baked from frozen. Proceed with Step 3, above, increasing baking time to 30 to 35 minutes.

Applesauce Carrot Muffins

MAKES 12 MUFFINS

This moist, not-too-sweet muffin can be packed in lunches or grabbed on the way out the door as a portable breakfast.

TIP

Cardamom lends a gingery spiciness to the muffins, but if unavailable, substitute cinnamon.

1 cup	all-purpose flour	250 mL
1 cup	whole wheat flour	250 mL
2 tsp	ground cardamom	10 mL
1 1/2 tsp	baking soda	7 mL
1/2 tsp	salt	2 mL
3/4 cup	packed brown sugar	175 mL
1/2 cup	vegetable oil	125 mL
2	eggs	2
1 cup	unsweetened applesauce	250 mL
1 1/2 cups	grated carrots (about 3)	375 mL
1/2 cup	raisins	125 mL

1. In a large bowl, stir together flours, cardamom, baking soda and salt.

2. In another bowl using an electric mixer, beat brown sugar with oil until blended. One at a time, beat in eggs. Beat in applesauce. Using wooden spoon, stir into flour mixture just until moistened. Stir in carrots and raisins. Spoon evenly into prepared muffin cups. *If freezing, see "to freeze" section below; otherwise proceed with Step 2.*

3. Preheat oven to 400° F (200° C). Bake muffins in center of oven for 18 to 20 minutes or until firm to the touch.

To freeze: Wrap muffin cups with heavy foil; seal, label and date. Freeze for up to 1 month.

To serve: Can be baked from frozen. Proceed with Step 3, above, increasing baking time to 30 to 35 minutes.

Big-Batch Bran Muffins

PREHEAT OVEN TO 375° F (190° C)
TWO 12-CUP MUFFIN TINS, GREASED OR PAPER-LINED

MAKES 24

5 cups	all-purpose flour	1.25 L
5 1/2 cups	100% bran cereal	1.375 L
2 cups	packed brown sugar	500 mL
1 cup	chopped dates or raisins	250 mL
1 tbsp	baking soda	15 mL
1 tbsp	cinnamon	15 mL
4 cups	buttermilk or sour milk (see Tip, at left)	1 L
1 cup	vegetable oil	250 mL
4	eggs	4

TIP

This batter can be prepared and stored for up to 2 weeks in the refrigerator. Pour batter into prepared muffin tins and bake as needed. Or you can bake the whole batch and keep extras in the freezer.

Sour milk can be used instead of buttermilk. To prepare, combine 3 tbsp (45 mL) lemon juice or white vinegar with 4 cups (1 L) milk and let stand for 5 minutes.

1. In a large bowl, combine flour, cereal, brown sugar, dates, baking soda and cinnamon.

2. In another large bowl, mix together buttermilk, oil and eggs. Stir into dry ingredients and mix until moistened.

3. Spoon batter into muffin cups, generously filling to the top. Bake in preheated oven for 25 to 30 minutes or until golden brown. Cool in pans for 5 minutes; remove muffins. Cool on a wire rack.

NUTRITION FACTS

Eating bran muffins for breakfast is a great way to get more fiber into your day. Wheat bran promotes regularity and a healthy digestive system.

From Dietitians of Canada: *Great Food Fast*

To freeze: When completely cool, wrap individually in plastic wrap, then overwrap with foil; seal, label and date. Freeze for up to 8 months.

To serve: Thaw in refrigerator overnight. Or pack frozen in a lunch bag to defrost by noon.

Cranberry Oatmeal Cookies

PREHEAT OVEN TO 350° F (180° C)
BAKING SHEETS, GREASED

MAKES 36

These cookies are quick to make, fun to eat and they're so easy that Bev's 10-year-old daughter Lisa can make them on her own.

TIP

Here's a tip from Ruby Bruce of South Lake, PEI: If you're looking for a supply of freshly baked cookies, make up a batch of your favorite cookie dough and bake some of your favorite cookies for immediate enjoyment. Form remaining cookie dough into small balls, place on cookie sheets and freeze. When frozen, put into a container and store in the freezer. Whenever you want a dozen freshly baked cookies, remove cookie balls from freezer, let thaw and bake.

VARIATION

Substitute 1/2 cup (125 mL) chocolate chips or your favorite chopped nuts for the dried cranberries. If using nuts, check for nut allergies before serving.

From Dietitians of Canada:
Great Food Fast

1 cup	all-purpose flour	250 mL
1/4 cup	wheat bran	50 mL
1/2 tsp	baking powder	2 mL
1/2 cup	margarine	125 mL
1/2 cup	granulated sugar	125 mL
1/2 cup	brown sugar	125 mL
1	egg	1
1 tsp	vanilla	5 mL
1 cup	quick-cooking (not instant) oats	250 mL
1/2 cup	dried cranberries	125 mL

1. In a small bowl, combine flour, wheat bran and baking powder. Set aside.

2. In a medium bowl, cream together margarine, granulated sugar and brown sugar until light and fluffy. Add egg and mix well; stir in vanilla. Add flour mixture and blend thoroughly. Stir in oats and cranberries.

3. Drop heaping teaspoons of cookie dough on prepared cookie sheets, about 2 inches (5 cm) apart. Bake in preheated oven for 10 to 12 minutes or until edges are lightly browned.

To freeze: When completely cool, transfer to freezer containers; seal, label and date. Freeze for up to 8 months.

To serve: Thaw in containers at room temperature.

Double Chocolate Chunk Cookies

**MAKES 3 1/2
DOZEN COOKIES**

Flecked with white chocolate chunks and walnuts, these fudgy cookies are a favorite with my family. Served with a cold glass of milk, they're pure heaven. I'm never short of taste testers when the first warm batch comes from the oven.

TIP

For perfectly baked cookies, place baking sheet on middle rack of oven; do only one sheet at time. Wipe baking sheets with paper towels or a damp cloth to remove grease. Also let sheets cool completely before using again to prevent dough from melting and spreading out too much during baking.

I like to double the recipe, bake half and freeze the remaining dough to bake another time.

PREHEAT OVEN TO 350° F (180° C)

3/4 cup	butter, softened	175 mL
3/4 cup	granulated sugar	175 mL
1/2 cup	packed brown sugar	125 mL
2	large eggs	2
2 tsp	vanilla	10 mL
1 1/2 cups	all-purpose flour	375 mL
1/2 cup	cocoa powder	125 mL
1/2 tsp	baking soda	2 mL
1/2 tsp	salt	2 mL
1 1/2 cups	white chocolate chunks	375 mL
1 cup	chopped walnuts or pecans	250 mL

1. In a large bowl, using an electric mixer, cream butter with granulated and brown sugars until fluffy; beat in eggs and vanilla until smooth.

2. In a separate bowl, sift together flour, cocoa powder, baking soda and salt. Beat into creamed mixture until combined; stir in white chocolate chunks and walnuts.

3. Drop tablespoonfuls (15 mL) of dough 2 inches (5 cm) apart on ungreased baking sheets.

4. Bake in preheated oven for 10 to 12 minutes or until edges are firm. (Bake for the shorter time if you prefer cookies with a soft chewy center.) Cool 2 minutes on baking sheets; remove to wire rack and cool completely.

Nothing ruins a cookie (or any other home-baked goods) more than rancid nuts, particularly walnuts. Taste before purchasing, if possible, to make sure nuts are fresh. Store them in a covered container in the fridge or freezer.

VARIATION

Omit cocoa powder; increase all-purpose flour to 1 3/4 cups (425 mL). Replace white chocolate chunks with semisweet chocolate chips.

From Johanna Burkhard: The *Comfort Food Cookbook*

To freeze: When completely cool, transfer to freezer containers; seal, label and date. Freeze for up to 8 months.

To serve: Thaw in containers at room temperature.

Buttermilk Pancakes with Spiced Maple Apples

MAKES ABOUT 18 PANCAKES

If I had to name one dish that brings my kids out from under their down comforters on a lazy weekend morning, this would be it. For a different twist, try these irresistible pancakes topped with spiced pear slices, too.

TIP

To keep pancakes warm, place on rack in warm oven.

Extra pancakes can be wrapped and frozen, then popped in the toaster for a quick breakfast.

To get a head start on a weekend breakfast, I measure out the dry ingredients for several batches of pancakes in advance, place in plastic bags and store in the cupboard. Beat in the liquid ingredients and the batter is ready for the griddle.

From Johanna Burkhard: The Comfort Food Cookbook

SPICED MAPLE APPLES

2 tbsp	butter	25 mL
4	apples or pears, peeled, cored and sliced	4
1/3 cup	maple syrup	75 mL
1/2 tsp	cinnamon	2 mL
1/2 tsp	ground ginger	2 mL
1/4 tsp	nutmeg	1 mL

PANCAKES

1 3/4 cups	all-purpose flour	425 mL
1 tbsp	granulated sugar	15 mL
2 tsp	baking powder	10 mL
1/2 tsp	baking soda	2 mL
1/2 tsp	salt	2 mL
2	large eggs	2
2 cups	buttermilk	500 mL
2 tbsp	melted butter	25 mL

1. Prepare the spiced maple apples: In a large nonstick skillet, melt butter over medium-high heat. Add apples, maple syrup, cinnamon, ginger and nutmeg; cook, stirring often, for 5 minutes or until apples are just tender. Keep warm.

2. In a bowl combine flour, sugar, baking powder, baking soda and salt. In another bowl, beat eggs; add buttermilk and melted butter. Whisk into flour mixture to make a smooth thick batter.

3. On an oiled griddle or in a large nonstick skillet over medium heat, drop quarter-cupfuls (50 mL) of batter and spread to a 4-inch (10 cm) circle. Cook for about 1 1/2 minutes or until bubbles appear on top; turn over and cook until browned on other side. *If freezing, see "to freeze" section below; otherwise proceed with Step 4.*

4. Serve with spiced maple apples.

To freeze: When completely cool, transfer apples and pancakes to separate freezer containers, layering pancakes with sheets of waxed paper; seal, label and date. Freeze for up to 2 months.

To serve: Thaw apples in refrigerator overnight. Thaw and heat pancakes, uncovered, in a 350° F (180° C) oven for 15 to 20 minutes or until warm. Proceed with Step 4, above.

a month of meals

Your freezer makes meal planning a snap. You can prepare foods a few days or weeks ahead – or, as this chart demonstrates, up to a full month in advance. Use these main-meal suggestions for brunch/lunch and dinner. Or choose your own favorites, adding any of the snack and dessert recipes in this book.

	SUNDAY	MONDAY	TUESDAY
WEEK 1	BRUNCH/LUNCH	LUNCH	LUNCH
	Chicken Frittata (page 89)	Fresh Tomato Dill Soup (page 78)	Taco Pitas (page 90)
	DINNER	DINNER	DINNER
	Easy Bouillabaisse (page 136)	Beef Bourguignon (page 110)	Chicken Tetrazzini (page 98)
	SUNDAY	**MONDAY**	**TUESDAY**
WEEK 2	BRUNCH/LUNCH	LUNCH	LUNCH
	Buttermilk Pancakes with Spiced Maple Apples (page 178)	Broccoli and Cheese-Stuffed Potatoes (page 50)	Hearty Tomato Vegetable Soup (page 79)
	DINNER	DINNER	DINNER
	Light 'n' Easy Chicken Tourtiere (page 142)	Best-Ever Meat Loaf) (page 92	Goulash (page 109) with Much More Mash (page 116)
	SUNDAY	**MONDAY**	**TUESDAY**
WEEK 3	BRUNCH/LUNCH	LUNCH	LUNCH
	Banana-Berry Wake-Up Shake (page 64) with Big-Batch Bran Muffins (page 174)	Salmon Sandwiches (page 84)	Cornish Pasty (page 86)
	DINNER	DINNER	DINNER
	Turkey Pot Pie with Biscuit Topping (page 102)	Pork and Chickpea Casserole (page 96)	Coq au Vin (page 114)
	SUNDAY	**MONDAY**	**TUESDAY**
WEEK 4	BRUNCH/LUNCH	LUNCH	LUNCH
	Whole Wheat Cheese Scones (page 156) with Strawberry Preserves (page 59)	Beef-Stuffed Spuds (page 48) (page 76)	Quick Chunky Minestrone
	DINNER	DINNER	DINNER
	Poppy Seed Noodle Casserole (page 105)	Pork Apple Curry (page 108)	Bavarian Stew (page 118)

WEDNESDAY	THURSDAY	FRIDAY	SATURDAY
LUNCH	LUNCH	LUNCH	LUNCH
Muffeletta (page 88)	Hearty Turkey Soup (page 73)	Hawaiian Tuna Wraps (page 85)	Ratatouille (page 82)
DINNER	DINNER	DINNER	DINNER
Chicken with Tarragon Herb Butter (page 56)	Pasta with Sausage and Tomato Sauce (page 123)	Chicken Chili Macaroni (page 104)	Meatloaf "Muffins" with Barbecue Sauce (page 91)

WEDNESDAY	THURSDAY	FRIDAY	SATURDAY
LUNCH	LUNCH	LUNCH	LUNCH
Chicken Tortellini Soup with Peas (page 75)	Herb-Filled Rolled Loaf (page 160)	Broccoli Soup with Tarragon (page 81)	Chicken Salad Niçoise (page 83)
DINNER	DINNER	DINNER	DINNER
Quick Chicken & Mushroom Pot Pies (page 100)	Carbonnade (page 112)	Chicken Shepherd's Pie (page 94)	Lazy Lasagna (page 97)

WEDNESDAY	THURSDAY	FRIDAY	SATURDAY
LUNCH	LUNCH	LUNCH	LUNCH
Ground Chicken Pizza (page 87)	Curried Parsnip and Pear Soup (page 80)	Green Beans Stewed with Tomatoes (page 51)	Pâté-Stuffed Baguette (page 133)
DINNER	DINNER	DINNER	DINNER
Fettuccine with Mushroom Cream Sauce (page 124)	Vegetarian Shepherd's Pie with Peppered Potato Topping (page 95)	Chicken and Broccoli Pasta with Pesto (page 106)	Baked Ham Fondue (page 93)

WEDNESDAY	THURSDAY	FRIDAY	SATURDAY
LUNCH	LUNCH	LUNCH	LUNCH
Sweet Onion and Tomato Soup (page 42)	Tuna Sandwiches (page 84)	Pea and Asparagus Soup with Fresh Tarragon (page 44)	Quick Chicken Noodle Soup (page 74)
DINNER	DINNER	DINNER	DINNER
Fish with Leek and Seafood Sauce (page 122)	Veal Stew with Dill and Mushrooms (page 107)	Veggie Beef and Pasta Bake (page 53)	Leek Soufflé (page 140)

INDEX